Confessions

Confessions

True-Life Revelations From
Radio 1's Breakfast Show

SIMON MAYO

Marshall Pickering
An Imprint of HarperCollins*Publishers*

First published in Great Britain in 1991
by Marshall Pickering

Marshall Pickering is an imprint of
HarperCollinsReligious
Part of HarperCollins*Publishers*
77–85 Fulham Palace Road, London W6 8JB

Printed and bound in Great Britain by
HarperCollinsManufacturing Glasgow

A catalogue record for this book is
available from the British Library

Contents

Introduction

Introductions to books are dull in the extreme; all full of tedious thank you's to friends, family, secretaries, without whom etc. . . . This is no different, but at least I will keep it to the end.

When 'Confessions' were first broadcast in the autumn 1990, I thought it would be a good little idea to run the Breakfast Show through to Christmas. It never occurred to me that they would still be going today, more popular than ever, or that they would end up on the front of the *Wall Street Journal* with every radio station in America trying to chase 'the crazy guy' who thought it up. 'Was I trying to challenge the power of the Catholic Church? What insight did it provide into the English psyche?' . . . Actually I told them rather unconvincingly, I fear all we are doing is having fun.

I receive about a hundred confessions a week and endeavour to read all of them. Obviously with only five shows a week most aren't used, but many would lead me and the BBC into deep water and legal action. Arson, divorce, torture, cruelty, infidelity and obscenity are just some of the topics we have covered – imagine what gets thrown out! I am not really suspicious, but it takes my dustman a half an hour to empty my bin!

Of course the rich and famous have as much, if not more, to confess to than Breakfast Show listeners. As and when they drop in, I ask for the odd juicy story. Paul Gascoigne admitted to cutting a fellow player's underwear, provoking the innocent player's wife to suspect a jealous lover. Gary Linekar came clean; he has always had his goody goody image, but while playing for his school team he got in such a foul temper over a disputed penalty, his dad persuaded the coach to substitute him. Most shocking of all was the inimitable Billy Connolly after a solid night's drinking, crashed out on a friend's bedroom floor, only waking up to find the desperate urge to find the bathroom. Being still 'half cut' this proved an impossibly difficult task, so he relieved himself in what he believed to be a vase on the mantelpiece. Two weeks later a letter from his drinking partner ('someone famous' says Billy), brings the appalling news that the vase, that had proved so convenient in his moment of need, was actually the last resting place of his flatmate's grandmother – yes it was an urn!

If that shocks you, this book is not for you. Put it down now for there is much more in the next few pages.

Here comes the boring bit. Heartfelt thanks have to go to Ric, Rod and Diane my bleary-eyed morning crew who make me sound good, to the Radio One Suits who take the angry calls from the 'stick insect protection action front', to my wife Hilary for suffering the 4.10 am alarm calls with such obvious enthusiasm, to James Grant Management and HarperCollins who guided these pages together and most of all to the Breakfast Show audience whose crimes I am only too happy to forgive – at £4.99 consider it a penance.

— 1 —

Childhood Innocence?

Without doubt one of the biggest files in my confessional is the one where forgivenesss is asked for 'because I was too young to know any better'. Whether it be feigning illness, defacing underwear, electrocuting your brother or defrauding John Noakes, childhood is, it seems, a good excuse for just about everything . . . .

Dear Simon,

I've been listening to the Confessions on your show since they started last year, and have just about built up enough courage to make my confession. I know full well that if either of my parents listen to your show, my life will be in great danger.

It was about ten years ago when I was nine, and the optician was visiting our school. I had a few friends who wore glasses and had noticed that due to their poor eyesight they often had to miss lessons to receive treatment. Being the 'dedicated' pupil that I was, I concluded that it would be a perfect opportunity to enhance my skiving career.

It was time for my eyes to be tested, and I 'unfortunately' was unable to read most of the chart or the reading book! This worried the optician, and she sent me straight away to the local hospital for more advanced tests. Here, similar results were found which totally baffled the specialist, because, as he explained, his apparatus indicated no weakness in either eye.

Over the next three years I travelled the country to see many of the top eye consultants. I had various scans with wires positioned all over my head and was prescribed bifocals and lots of other categories of 'milk bottles'.

Then, my eyes miraculously recovered and I no longer needed any glasses. None of the surgeons could explain why!

Now I confess that during those three years nothing at all was wrong with my eyesight, except perhaps being tired of looking at classroom walls.

I beg forgiveness, via your crew, from the eye specialists and mainly from my parents who spent three years worrying about the undiscovered eye disease I had, and transporting me all over the country.

I have since been punished slightly because I now have to wear contact lenses all the time.

Please forgive me,
Jane.

Dear Darling Twiglet-legs,

HELP! I have a dark and murky secret lurking in my dim and distant past, and I badly need to repent. If I do not unburden my soul soon, then I shall be driven completely around the twist by the suspense of wondering what my family's reactions will be when they finally discover the hidden skeleton in my cupboard . . .

It happened ten years ago, in the summer holidays, when I was nine. My Mum, my sister and I all went off to stay with my Nan, and, as luck would have it, my Nan's sister was also staying there – Great Auntie Elsie (GAE). You know what it's like when you're little: you go out shopping and end up spending half the day hanging about in the street because some ancient old lady stops to talk to you. Even if you think you've never seen her before, she raves on about how cute you used to look sitting in your pram sucking a dummy!

Anyway, on this particular occasion I was really fed up. The entire day had been wasted and we only had enough time to go into one more shop before they all shut. GAE wanted to treat herself to a new pair of drawers – we are not talking normal simple drawers here, we are talking *megaknickers* – the ever so gorgeous woolly sort which reach down to your knees! Well, after ages deciding which ones to buy, we eventually went home.

Later on that evening, when everybody was watching TV, I just happened to be passing GAE's bedroom, and what do you think were sitting on the bed still in the brown paper bag? Yes! You've guessed! Such a delicate shade of peach, the white frilly lace was very fetching, so attractive, so alluring, so . . .

I had a nice new biro in my hand, and suddenly I was taken by some mysterious force. Before I knew what was happening I had written a very appropriate message on the left cheek – 'I ♥ SEX'!! I don't know what came over me, honestly!!

Well, as you can imagine, there were fireworks when my artistic graffiti was discovered. Luckily, while we were all rolling around on the floor with laughter (apart from the unlucky victim, who was screeching,

'I'm disgusted, it's an outrage!'), nobody noticed the twinkling in my innocent eyes. The next day we marched back to the shop and demanded to see the manager, who promised to interrogate all the staff. It was eventually deduced that the Saturday girl had gone a bit wild when pricing the delightful garment, so she was promptly sent off to price knickers in the job centre!

To this day no one suspects me in the slightest, but I feel that the time has come to confess. Perhaps I will now be able to get dressed in the morning without smirking! I only hope that GAE is not listening, or I'm likely to be exiled to some remote part of the globe!

Am I forgiven?

Yours faithfully,
A poor student, who you may call Dummy!

Dear Simon, Rod and Diane,

Please hear my confession about a 'mishap' which has weighed heavy on my troubled mind for a number of years. I'm twenty-five now and reasonably grown up, although some might argue that point because of a somewhat, shall we say, 'alternative' sense of humour.

My confession goes back to the time when I was around seven years of age. I was dragged out shopping by my mother one packed Saturday morning and, like most mothers, mine used to stand and chat to friends for ages leaving the hapless child (i.e. me) holding on to her hand feeling thoroughly bored. Anyway, she'd stopped to talk to this woman in one of the local stores, rather close to the top of the escalator.

Having stood there for around ten minutes getting totally cheesed off and being told about forty times to stand still/stop fidgeting, I spied something which struck me as a potential source of amusement. There, tucked away at the top of the escalator under the rotating rubber hand rail was a red circle which said 'Emergency Stop'.

A swift calculation in my devious little mind sussed that I could reach this red circle using the tip of my umbrella without bringing any unnecessary attention my way. Bearing in mind that this escalator was reasonably full and could possibly cause quite serious injury, I pushed the button.

Instead of grinding to a steady halt this thing hurled the unsuspecting shoppers to the floor with a commendable amount of G-Force. It was chaos! Grannies were headbutting the people directly in front of them, and those menacing shopping baskets on wheels that most old folk have (usually in tartan) were demonstrating their remarkable hidden talents at administering puncture wounds.

Mother, my mother's friend and I looked on in horror (or mock horror in my case). The icing on the cake to this tale is that amidst all this pandemonium, at the bottom of the stairs could be seen a young lad being given the slapping of his life by his irate mother (one of those mothers whose every word was accompanied by a sharp clout), who was screaming, 'What have I told you before about touching things that don't belong to you?'

Do you think I could possibly be forgiven?

Lots of Love,
F.

Dear Simon and the crew,

My true confession happened ten years ago when I was twelve years old.

Dad, who had just come out of hospital after having his appendix taken out, was recovering at home. My brother, Steven, who was ten, Mum and I were all in the bedroom watching TV and having coffee and biscuits. Anyway, the biscuits were Lincolns, the ones with pimples on, and after we had eaten a few, my brother went to get another one and found the pimples were all red – the same on another three in the packet.

So Mum sent the packet back to the manufacturer. Two weeks later, a man came to our house full of apologies, and with a load of free products. He explained that the lab technicians had been carrying out tests on the biscuits. The staff had been quizzed, but that they were all baffled by it.

Well now I confess to Mum, and the baffled technicians, that it was me who had previously removed them from the packet and coloured them in with a felt tip pen. Sorry, everyone. Please forgive me!

Yours truthfully,
Paul.F.

Dear Father Mayo,

Bless me Father for I have sinned, and no amount of visits to the confession box will help, for I have caused my sister no end of misery!

You see, when Libby was born back in 1971, she messed up my cosy set up. My elder sister, Twink, was Dad's little girl, and I was Mum's baby – and then Mother produced this wrinkly blob that poo-poohed and puked all day and took up so much of everybody's time that I got jealous. To make matters worse the 'blob' became a resident in my bedroom; and, as the saying goes, 'hell hath no fury like a woman scorned' – especially a four year old!!

Anyway, as the 'blob' grew, I plotted revenge for being pushed out of the limelight. I not only sat on Libby when she needed a wee and made her wet the bed, but on one occasion when the poor lamb was about three, I told her to call Daddy a 'bastard', because he would love her for saying it as it meant he was a 'nice man'. Needless to say, Dad was mortified and Libby was very nearly liquidised.

However, my biggest, worsest, nastiest sin is that I told the poor girl she was adopted because she was such an ugly baby that nobody wanted her, so Mum and Dad had taken her in out of pity. I really played on this, and although she tried to laugh it off, it did hurt her – and she still brings it up in conversation now, so it must have had a big effect.

As she and her boyfriend are about to embark on a year-long world trip, I feel compelled to write and ask for forgiveness for being such a bad sister and to clear my conscience before she goes.

Libby, I really am truly sorry, and I hope you can forgive me for being so horrible to you. I hope you both have a memorable trip – see you next year!

Father Mayo, I thank you for helping me. Now I've got all that off my chest, I can sleep peacefully.

Love,
Pig (in-the-middle).

P.S. Please also say a humungous sorry to Nigel (he knows who he is) – and tell him I miss him desperately despite what I said, but that's a different story!!

Dear Simon,

After listening to your show each day, I have decided I simply have to get off my chest an incident I've felt absolutely awful about for years.

I'm twenty-one and am a self-employed decorator. About six years ago, when waking up for school, late as usual, I noticed my brother, who is a chef, had overslept too. After I had woken him up, he talked me into bunking off school for the day and going down to the pub with him instead.

Off I trundled to school, signed the late book outside the Headmaster's office, and then tiptoed off to the pub to meet my brother. Three hours and six or seven pints later, we decided to have a stumble around town. We wound up in the car-park of the telephone exchange (where my father worked as a security guard), and quietly relieved ourselves in the corner.

Our father was due to finish work any minute, and just for a laugh I decided to let down the tyres of his car. Then we hid in the doorway of a nearby shop.

We were unable to contain ourselves as my father, after a hard day's work, came towards his car and noticed both front tyres were flat. After turning green and then white he kicked the door of his brand new Fiat Strada, leaving a perfect imprint of his foot in the door of his pride and joy. Needless to say, we scarpered!

I still see the pain in his face as he sees Fiat Stradas around town, and then proceeds to heap curses and insults on the two little brats who were seen letting down his tyres, causing him to boot his beloved car. So, from Patch and Skip (that's us – we're not a couple of Labradors), I'd like to say, 'Sorry, Dad. We never meant it.'

Yours sincerely,
'Patch'.

Simon Mayo
Confessions
Radio 1

Dear Simon,

I would like to confess to something which happened quite a few years ago, when my brother and I lived in Glasgow.

It was a Friday night and we were due to go and stay with my grandmother in London the next day for our summer holiday. My mum was out shopping and my brother had a few friends round from school to say goodbye.

We had a very old-fashioned kitchen with a big range. Above the range was a line where my mum had hung all our undies to air ready for us to take on our hols. Also hanging on the line was my mum's pride and joy, a beautiful pink petticoat, the type worn in those days, made of the stuff that made your dress stick out when you sat down. It was lovely, with lots of lace and pink rosebuds. Well, my brother, who was fifteen at the time, and his friends were in the kitchen – I wasn't allowed in, being much younger, so I spied on them through the crack in the door. I could see them playing with the poker attached to the gas cooker, and burning bits of string which I thought was very naughty of them. I decided I would tell my mum.

My brother decided that it was time everyone went home and while they were getting their coats on, I decided to have a go at lighting the poker myself. There I was, gaily waving this flame about when all of a sudden – whoosh! My mum's lovely pink petticoat was melting on to the floor. I put the poker back and ran down to the front door and said 'I can smell something burning, can't you?' They all sniffed and ran down to the kitchen, where by now all our underclothes were alight.

Imagine the scene. You have just picked up your wife from outside the supermarket after having had a hard day at the office to be greeted by a number of frantic teenagers carrying buckets and bowls of burning socks, ties and various other assortments of underwear to the bathroom. Well, my mum screamed and my dad blew a gasket. After a frantic half hour, they had the situation under control. My brother said a sheepish 'goodbye' to his friends, and then we were interrogated. As I didn't want to get smacked and I didn't particularly want to get my brother into too much trouble, I decided that I would blame his friend Steven, who I didn't really like anyway. I said that I saw him playing with the poker in the kitchen and to my surprise my brother backed me up.

Well the end of the story is that Steven got banned for life from the house, my brother was grounded for quite some time and me – well I got a whole load of new underclothes.

This incident has always been on my mind and I'd just like to say 'sorry' to Steven, wherever he is, to my brother and my parents, especially my mum who was so upset at having lost her beautiful petticoat – not even the elastic was left – but she did get a new kitchen out of it.

Barbara.

Dear Simon,

I have a dreadful confession to make. Seven years ago, aged thirteen, I used to live in a cul-de-sac. My friends who lived in the street used to get up to various pranks, but nothing compared to what happened on a hot summer's day in 1984. It hadn't rained for weeks and we were sitting on a grass bank, wondering what mischief we could get up to.

Finally, one of the gang, Gary, suggested that we light a fire. This went down well, so we each went home to collect items to burn. I went over to call on James, a friend of mine who had just arrived home from the shops. Unfortunately, he wasn't allowed out because of an incident at the supermarket (probably another confession there!), so I trudged back to the chosen spot for the fire.

We piled the old newspapers and litter together and poured on some oil. Before long, we had a nice blaze going. However, when we added more oil to it, it started to get out of control. We tried to put the fire out, but only succeeded in setting a nearby conifer alight. As it erupted, we realised that we were in trouble and we ran off. I found my mother, told her that there was a fire across the road. While she rang the emergency number, I looked out of the window and watched the flames envelop the end of a neighbour's garden.

At this point, James, having been sent to his room, looked out of his window and saw the fire. He shinned down the drainpipe outside his bedroom window and rushed towards the fire with the blanket from his bed. He threw it over the blaze and jumped back as it too went up in flames.

As he tried desperately to put out the fire, it reached the caravan parked in the neighbour's garden, and it was soon burning furiously too. At this point, a fire engine and a police car arrived. The policeman grabbed James and pulled him towards the car, obviously thinking that James had started it. Unfortunately for James, a number of people had seen him burning a blanket and this only served to confirm the policeman's suspicions.

The fireman finally put out the fire just before the neighbour's house caught fire, but his caravan was completely destroyed. Since James was only ten at the time, he got away with a severe warning from the police and a punishment from his parents.

To this day, James does not know how the fire started, but now that the neighbour has gone, I feel it is the right time to confess our pyromaniac activities. Will James and the Crew forgive us?

Yours sincerely,
Dave.

Dear Simon,

I'm so glad that you have started a confessional service, because it allows me to admit something I did which I've never had the courage to confess before.

Some twelve years ago, I did an awful thing. You see, being the grand old age of ten, I felt that my bicycle was too small and babyish for me. To give you some idea what this bike was like, it was called a 'Zippy' – yes, that's right, after the character in Rainbow.

Well, I nagged and nagged my parents for a new bike, but to no avail. Their argument was that there was nothing wrong with the one I had, and I could wait a few years before I got a new one.

All I could think about was getting a new bike, so I decided to take things into my own hands. My younger sister was only a baby and once a week I was sent to the shops at the end of our road to fetch baby milk. On one such visit, I noticed that behind the shops it was very overgrown with weeds and nettles about knee high. An idea formed in my mind.

Bit by bit I began to dismantle my bike. Each week a nut or bolt or screw would mysteriously disappear, until finally, one day, I arrived home pushing what was left of my bike. I pretended to be most distraught and told my parents that somehow my bike had just simply fallen apart. I must have been convincing because they believed me.

Sure enough, my wicked plan worked and a week later I was presented with a brand new 'grown-up' bike. I feel really awful about this now and I've never admitted what terrible lengths I went to so I could get a new bike. We have since moved, but if they ever develop the piece of land behind the shops, they will come across enough parts of a bike to build a new one!

I'm sorry, Mum and Dad. I hope I can be forgiven.

from
Karen.

Dear Simon, Rod and Diane,

I too have to write and beg forgiveness.

When I was little, I was a great fan of Blue Peter. I regularly wrote letters and sent pictures to Valerie, John and Peter, and was rewarded with photos of them all including Shep and Freda.

I had recently planted an apple pip out of my freshly eaten apple – and fully expected an apple tree to sprout immediately.

After a few weeks, I grew bored with the lack of progress so I substituted the apple pip with a sycamore seedling out of our garden. The new seedling thrived and soon the sapling was a foot tall.

I proudly wrote to Valerie, John and Peter about my apple tree grown from a seed. In return I received a much-coveted Blue Peter badge. All my school friends were most impressed at this status symbol.

Unfortunately the tree was thriving so well it started producing leaves . . . sycamore leaves which rather gave the game away! My mum was furious and confiscated my Blue Peter badge for lying!

Do you think Biddy Baxter would ever forgive me if she knew?

Then again, would you?

Love,
Sue.

Dear Simon, Oxers, Rob and Producer of the Day,

I have a confession that's been on my mind for twelve years and I think it's time I told all.

When I was five and my brother was four, we shared a room. In this room was only one electric plug socket, but it was covered by a piece of wood.

One day, my brother and I tried to see what was behind the wood. We had a pair of scissors with a plastic handle and I put the scissors down behind the wood. There was a big bang and all the electricity in the house went off.

My dad rushed up to our room, and thanks to my quick thinking (even at five), I handed the scissors to my brother! My dad saw him with the scissors, and smacked him and sent him to bed.

Please can you forgive me?

Mike (aged seventeen).

Witton, Birmingham

Dear Simon and Co,

I've done plenty of wrong things in my time, but there is only one that I feel really guilty about.

I was about ten, and my brother, Kevin, would have been six. It wasn't long after Christmas, Mum and Dad had bought Kevin a space hopper that year, and to save having to blow it up and let it down all the time it was kept in the only space available – the airing cupboard.

I don't know what possessed me, but each time I went to the airing cupboard and looked at this space hopper, my fingertips started to itch and I had naughty thoughts!

I had to put myself out of my misery. So one day I took a pin, and strolled to the airing cupboard. Instead of sticking it completely through the hopper, my conscience only allowed me to prick the surface.

I went to bed that evening feeling relieved and secretly thinking I wouldn't have pricked it hard enough to harm it anyway.

The next day my poor little brother ran to the cupboard, full of excitement and eager to play on his space hopper. Only it had shrunk. The tears on his face and the look of disappointment were too much for me to bear – I hid that day. Mum consoled Kevin and explained that he'd probably space-hopped on some broken glass somewhere.

Well, Kev, it'll be your twenty-first birthday in December, and I promise I'll get you a space hopper just like the one you had which I destroyed.

I've never been to confession before, but I feel a lot better now. I may start making this confession lark a habit!

Yours sincerely,
Jenny.

— 2 —

Happy Families

Without brothers and sisters, mums, dads, wives, husbands, in-laws and kids is it any wonder that the family nest is such a fruitful area for confessions? On the subject of fruit, look out for one of my favourites, the Christmas pudding from Down Under. Everyone has a confession in this field – it's just that the following confessees are more honest than you.

Father Simon
Radio 1 Confessional
London W1A 4WW

Dear Father Simon,

I have a confession to make which is so shameful I have not got the courage to give you my name.

One lazy family Sunday afternoon, my eldest brother got out his recent family holiday snaps. Being very bored, I flicked through them quickly. I was intrigued to find that only seventeen photographs had come out, so I studied the negatives to find out what had gone wrong.

Imagine my surprise when I realised all twenty-four photographs had in fact come out, but seven had been removed from the batch! These photographs were of my brother's wife in various states of undress. I slyly pocketed these negatives, and handed the holiday snaps back to my brother.

The next day, I nipped down to the chemist and had some copies of the saucy photos made up. I then sent them off to one of those national magazines, entering them in the 'Readers' Wives' section.

Well, several weeks passed before I was summoned to a family conference along with my two other brothers. Father interrogated us three while our eldest brother looked on. In one hand he held a copy of the magazine in which his wife appeared as 'Julie from Newcastle' – and in his other hand he held a cheque from the magazine for £50.00 for the use of the photographs.

I managed to plead my innocence and finally one of my other brothers was accused.

I hope both of my brothers can forgive me although I dare not let them know.

Yours,
Anon.

Dear Simon,

This confession makes me shake everytime I think of it. I hope you can forgive me. It goes back to a festive season of my youth. We didn't get our usual Christmas presents from Uncle Ernie and Auntie Sheila in Australia, but then a mysterious pot of exotic-smelling herbs and spices arrived from Oz.

Mum put them in the Christmas pud and it tasted great. We ate half and kept the rest in the fridge.

A week later we heard from Auntie Sheila that Uncle Eric had died and had we received his ashes to bury in Britain.

Fortunately our father is a Minister so we were able to have a little service of interment for the remainder of the pudding, or should that be the remains of Uncle Eric?

We are really sorry; we wouldn't have eaten Uncle Eric if we'd known. Can we be forgiven?

The Wilkinsons.

Dear Simon,

Every morning, on our way to work in the car, my boyfriend and I take great pleasure in turning the radio up and listening to other people's evil misdeeds on your confessional spot. However, I feel that the time has come for my boyfriend, Richard, to confess, for the first time, to something he and his elder brother did quite a few years ago. So I am confessing on his behalf!

Richard and Steve's oldest brother, Aiden, had just joined the police force, and proud with his first wage packet, he bought himself a little Viva car. He loved that car, Simon. He would wash and wax it every week; it was his pride and joy. Being his first car, it would be, wouldn't it?

Now, when Aiden came home one morning from a tiring night shift, he put his keys on the table and went to bed. It was at this point that Steve, then sixteen, said to Richard, who was then fourteen, 'Let's take Aiden's car out for a spin.'

So that's just what they did. They collected all their friends and went for a drive. They were having great fun until they hit the corner of a pavement and the car turned over.

Oh dear! Quickly the lads got out of the car and pushed it back on to its wheels, only to find that the front wheel had buckled under and the car was impossible to drive. So Richard and Steve had to run about four miles home before Aiden woke up and before their mother and father came in.

Nothing was said until Aiden got up to go back to work. When he found that his car was missing, Richard and Steve stayed stum about what had happened of course, and Aiden had to phone the police and report his car stolen.

His car was found eventually, with the front wheel buckled, and Steve (who was training to be a car mechanic) offered to fix the car (for a small fee of course). Aiden was very grateful for this.

Aiden still doesn't know about all this; do you think he'll find it in his heart to forgive them now, nearly ten years later? And also, could you apologise to the police for wasting their time, Simon?

Yours hopefully,
Joanna.

Simon Mayo
Radio 1

Dear Simon and Team,

After listening to the True Confessions of others, I felt that I had to write to bare my soul, hoping at last to free myself from the burden of guilt that I have carried for the last four years.

I was living with my Aunt Margaret in Stubbins, Lancashire, and had been left in charge of the family home after my parents had moved to Norfolk. I had stayed on in Lancashire because we had decided I should finish my schooling – I was sixteen, in my final year at school, and taking exams.

My family were sending me a monthly allowance, some for me and some for Aunt Margaret for looking after me. But I was sixteen, discovering life and my allowance was soon used up. So, finding myself skint, what was I to do?

At this moment I would like to ask my parents, 'What do you think happened to the two bikes (mine and my sister's), the drill and the building tools? The very same items that you searched the house and garden for, and finally claimed for on the insurance?'

Well, both bikes went to a mate, and the drill and building tools went

to a mate's mate's dad's mate. These items made a total of £85, and I was able once more to enjoy the style of life to which I had become accustomed.

I would like to apologise to my parents, my sister and the insurance company, and all I can offer in my defence is that when you're young and living life in the fast lane, you have to take chances.

Yours sincerely,
C.R.H.

P.S. I was also offered £15 for the washer/dryer, but I thought that wasn't enough.

Dear Simon and the crew,

I have been listening to your 'Confessions' slot for quite a while now and have finally plucked up enough courage to bare my soul to the world in general, and my wife in particular, regarding a wind-up which went wrong. We'll call my wife Mary Jones for the sake of secrecy.

In 1987 I secretly bought two tickets for a Dave Bowie concert at Roker Park football ground in Sunderland, and also arranged for Mary to have a day off work on the day of the concert – I even set the clock two hours back so that she could have a lie in – how thoughtful! On the morning of the fateful day, when Mary eventually woke up, I told her that I was going to take her out but did not tell her where – how romantic!!

Anyway, while Mary was getting ready, I thought of a brilliant wind-up and this is what I did:

At that time, we were not on the phone, which actually helped the plot. I went round to the nearest payphone (which by some strange quirk of fate was working), rang Mary's workplace, put on a phoney voice and asked to speak to her, knowing full well that she was not there. The receptionist put me through to her extension and Mary's workmate (who we'll call Sue) answered the phone, as per the plot.

Using my phoney voice I asked her if Mary Jones was available and she naturally said no – she's on a day's holiday (Sue knew that I was taking Mary to the concert).

I then told Sue that I worked for Readers' Digest promotions and that Mary had won £50,000 in a prize draw but she had to claim it by noon today or she would forfeit it (it was already 11.30 a.m.). Sue told me that unfortunately Mary was not on the phone but she would see what she could do.

I then put the phone down, went home and whisked Mary off to the concert before anything could be done about contacting her – a perfect stitch-up – or so I thought.

We had a great time at the concert and I went to bed that night sound in the knowledge that Mary was going to be well wound up the next day.

The next day, we both went back to work and I waited for the plot to thicken, which it did drastically. Mary rang me at my workplace in some distress and told me about the man from Readers' Digest – great, I thought, it's worked.

Then she told me that when Sue had put the phone down she rang The Readers' Digest back, who denied any knowledge of a £50,000 prize draw.

Sue then rang my sister and told her the tale and they both came to the conclusion that something funny was going on. My sister then thought that someone could have been checking up on us to see if we were in with a view to burgling the house (by now we were probably having a drink in Sunderland) so she decided to phone the police, who nicely kept a watch on the house for me all day!

What a disaster – everything had gone wrong and it was me that ended up in a state.

The only saving grace is that I did not have to deny being a part of this dastardly deed, as no one bothered to ask if I was involved.

Will my wife ever forgive me?
Will 'Sue' ever forgive me?
Will my sister ever forgive me?
Will the Readers' Digest ever forgive me?
Will the police ever find me?

Yours,
Concerned.

West Sussex

BBC Radio 1
Simon Mayo's Breakfast Show
True Confessions
London
W1A 4WW

Dear Simon,

After years of torment I have decided to confess to you my dreadful deed. It happened at Christmas eight years ago.

My family and I were then living in a large house in the countryside. The house had land, stables, horses, gravel drive, etc. My father commuted up to London on the train every day, leaving his brand new, extremely expensive car parked safely on the drive. (Or, at least, he thought it was safe!)

One day, over the school Christmas holiday, I was bored with riding my horse and decided a spin in Dad's car was just what I needed for a bit of excitement. Before I knew it, I was racing up and down the gravel drive doing handbrake turns, and thoroughly enjoying myself. Unfortunately, as my confidence grew so did the pressure of my foot on the accelerator! The car's rear end skidded around, totally out of control, and there was a horrible sound of metal and glass meeting a low brick wall.

The wall was only a foot and a half high and on inspection I was amazed that such a little wall could cause such a lot of damage. By now I was starting to realise the seriousness of my actions and what Dad was going to say. So, I parked the car *exactly* where I had found it, decided I was coming down with a fever, and went to my bedroom. (Might as well – I'd only be sent there anyway!)

My Dad came home, and then went straight out again – down to the local Rugby Club, of which he was the President, because it was their Christmas bash. I assumed that he had not noticed the damage and would probably see it only when he got out of the car at the club.

But I tossed and turned all night in bed.

At breakfast the next morning, my father appeared looking a little upset. We enquired as to his well-being, and it turned out that Mark – one of the young Rugby players – had managed to reverse into the car, and it now had a nasty dent. The whole family trooped outside to inspect the damage (even me, who by this stage suddenly had a nice warm feeling of well-being and relief).

Yes! I looked at the car and it looked exactly as it had done the evening before when I parked it . . . dented!

I would like to take this opportunity to say thank you to Mark, who ended up paying for it, and that I am truly, truly sorry. Also to my father, 'Dad, I'm sorry but with the amount of pocket money you used to give me, it would have taken about three years to pay it off!'

Yours sincerely,
Dee xx.

Newport
Gwent

Dear Simon,

I'm afraid I can't reveal my full name, since it could cost me dear. This confession goes back to last summer, when my father had a new computer system fitted in his offices.

One Friday lunchtime, my mother asked me to drive to the office because Dad had phoned to say he'd left his wallet at home. I drove over but found that the office door was locked. Luckily, I had a key and I went upstairs. The office was deserted. Maybe the office computer would explain where everyone was.

I turned on a monitor and pressed a few keys. Nothing seemed to happen. I played around for a few minutes, when suddenly a message appeared on the screen. It said 'Abort, Yes/No?' I typed 'Yes' and the screen went blank. I got up hurriedly and turning off the monitor, I turned to leave. As I left, I noticed a sign on the back of the door which said, 'Gone for lunch at Terry's'.

I soon found out that all the office staff were out to lunch to celebrate the completion of the computer system and its connection to the computer systems of ten other branches of the firm. I gave Dad the wallet and left.

That evening, Dad came home in a huge temper. Apparently someone in his branch had wiped out the whole computer file – not just in his branch, but in another six branches around the country as well. The cost for all the repairs would be almost £4,000.

Needless to say, I've kept quiet for some months but feel that I can confess now. I hope I have your forgiveness!

Yours beggingly,
David.

Purton
Wiltshire

Dear Simon and Breakfast Crew,

I just had to write to you after your Breakfast Show Confessions prompted my brother, Mark, to confess all, thereby solving one of life's mysteries!

To explain: the story starts in 1981, when I had just purchased a brand new Honda 90 motorbike. After only three months, the bike continually broke down, resulting in many heated rows with the supplier – who reluctantly had to provide a full refund.

No more thought was given to the problem until recently, when my brother, Mark, confessed that, while I was asleep after a night shift, he'd taken the motorbike for a scrambling session with some friends along the canal bank. Yes – you've guessed it – the motorbike ended up in the canal, which damaged all the electrics. This explains the constant breakdowns.

So your confessions spot has cleared up that little mystery. Not that it has made much difference to my relationship with my now deceased (only joking) brother.

I enjoy the show and all the crew, especially the lovely Diane – can she blow me a kiss?

Many thanks,
Colin.

— 3 —

The Happiest Days
of Your Life

The frightening thing about this book is that it might just conceivably fall into the wrong hands. I certainly wouldn't want any child of mine to read the next few tales of debauchery, bullying, deception and torture. School, it seems, brings out the best and worst of everyone . . . .

Dear Simon,

I have been kept awake at night worrying about the awful thing I used to do to a girl who was in my class when I was five years old. Her name was Vivien and as this happened fourteen years ago I'm hoping that she'll forgive me!

Every morning, we had an assembly, and Vivien used to stand in front of me. One morning, I found that I had no hankie, so instead of suffering a blocked nose, I picked my nose and wiped it on the back of Vivien's jumper! After that, every time I found myself in the same situation, I used Vivien's jumper!

So you see, Vivien, the children weren't laughing at my runny nose after all; they were laughing at the growing stock-pile stuck to the back of your jumper! I'm sorry for the years of misery that I so obviously put you through.

Yours in hope,
Lisa.

Dear Simon,

It all happened in the Lower Sixth. I had a best friend called Alan. We were always finding ways of playing practical jokes on each other. But when it ended in Alan getting me suspended for two weeks, we decided enough was enough. However, I was still out for revenge!

One day, I was round at Alan's and we were sitting in the kitchen when someone said, 'Who's a pretty boy, then?' I looked around the room and saw a parrot in a cage by the back-door window. Alan told me that he was looking after the parrot for the next-door neighbours, a very posh Irish couple who had gone back to Ireland for a few weeks.

Alan was pleased with this Panamanian parrot, as it would repeat everything he said (if he said it enough times).

Then it slowly dawned on me what I would do!

Every day, in my lunch hour, I went to Alan's and climbed over the fence to get round to the back of the house. I found that the top part of the kitchen window was always open and so my revenge began!

I dictated to the parrot some of my worse, most offensive Irish jokes. I did this every day for two weeks. Alan didn't catch on – he heard the parrot say some weird stuff sometimes, but he thought it was just his own family being repeated.

When the Irish couple came back home, and collected the parrot, I left Alan's house in rather a hurry!

The next day in school, Alan had a broken nose. He told me he didn't understand why! He thought he'd done a very good job of looking after the parrot! But the Irish couple didn't!

I have never confessed this, and to this day Alan doesn't know why this

Irish couple acted so badly towards him.

By the way – they got rid of the parrot a few days later!

So sorry to the parrot – hope it's got a good home with someone who likes Irish jokes.

Sorry to the couple next door – no offence meant.

And most of all,

Sorry to Alan, whose nose didn't fix straight, and still has a crook in it – please forgive me!

Anon.

P.S. Please read this out, because I can't tell Alan to his face, but I know he listens.

Simon Mayo
BBC Radio 1 FM
LONDON

Dear Father Mayo,

My confession goes back to 1983 when Mandy, Ian, Lisa, Andrew, Alan and I were all in the same class at school.

We all used to mate round together, and so we usually went into dinner together. It didn't matter what dinner was, Alan would always be ready to eat any of our left-overs! He was the same in the playground, and when we sneaked food into class he was always asking for some of our snacks. After a while we all began to get fed up with this, so we decided to teach him a lesson.

So, every afternoon for a week, Mandy came back in after break eating a chocolate bar and, sure enough, Alan always asked her if he could have some, but she'd always say no. Then on the Friday afternoon, as we came back in from break, Alan asked Mandy if he could have some of her chocolate and she said yes. Alan was absolutely made up at the thought of getting his teeth into the lovely chocolate.

We all went into class giggling and laughing and feeling thoroughly pleased with ourselves. The reason for us all feeling so smug was that, just before Alan had asked Mandy for her chocolate, we had swapped it for a bar of laxative chocolate.

He sat through the last lesson sneaking it out of his coat pocket and eating it. Even when he had finished it, all he could say to Mandy was, 'I don't really like plain; I prefer milk instead.' On hearing this, we all burst out laughing and went our separate ways home.

After a thoroughly smug weekend, we all went back to school on the Monday, only to find that Alan hadn't turned up. After the register had been called we decided to ask our teacher why Alan was off. She told us that Alan's mum had rung in to say Alan hadn't been very well at the weekend, but that as soon as he was better he'd be back in school.

He didn't come back to school for nearly two weeks because he was so ill.

Father Mayo, do you think we can be forgiven for putting Alan through this terrible ordeal.

Yours begging for absolution on behalf of four others as well,
Donna.

Dear Simon,

My name is Flora! (*I am too embarrassed to reveal my true identity!*)

My confession goes back to when I was in infant school somewhere in West Yorkshire.

Every odd afternoon we had to do Sums, and me being about as mathematically minded as Gazza hated these little sessions! I wanted to play in the Wendy House and pretend to play pubs (*I started early!*).

I had to find a way to get out of doing sums. So one afternoon I master-minded a plan. Sneaking a wax crayon in my Charlies Angels' catsuit pocket, I wandered over to the teacher with a desperate look on my face and asked if I could please go to the toilet. Once in the toilet I got the crayon out and started to scribble on the walls and on the floor! When I had finished, with an evil little giggle and a spring in my step, I bounded down to the Headmistress's office to tell her that some scallywag had scribbled in one of the toilets (snigger snigger) and would she like me to try to clean it off (snigger snigger)?

Well I was immediately made 'Clean-up the Crayola' monitor, thus getting out of Sums, plus when I finished I was rewarded with Spangles! What a scam! I remember wondering why criminals got caught; it was so easy to get away with these things!

These little vandalising sessions happened quite frequently, I used to ask to go for a widdle but really I'd go and scribble!!!

I never did get caught, but I think that always being the one to find the scribbling put me as a suspect!!

After leaving school at 16 with an 'X' for my maths, I look back with sorrow.

Do you think I will be forgiven?

Will you all forgive me?

Yours hopefully,
Flora,
The Phantom Scribbler of 4H!

Dear Simon,

Back in the good old days of 'O' levels, before Mrs T was in power, this saga erupted.

It was two days before the Parents' Evening, and like normal it had been a very bad term for me. I was on the way to hand some books in, and on the teacher's desk there was a big blue book. It was the mark book!

There was no one in the room, so I decided to have a little look. My highest marks were an 'F', and 13% (unlucky for some!!).

Then it occurred to me, I could change a few marks. The 'F' could be easily changed to a 'B', and the 13% to 73%.

When my parents got home from the Parents' Evening, they said that they had a surprise for me. The next day they took me down to 'Billy's Bikes' and bought me a shining new Raleigh bike!

I wish to confess to my parents because they spent half my Dad's wage on me when I didn't deserve it.

Will you forgive me?

Signed,
John Smith.

Dear Simon,

I am writing to confess! When I was at junior school, aged between seven and ten years, I was quite near to being a perfect 'role-model' pupil – or so the teachers thought. Always willing to help, always well presented, never answering back, and giving the teacher little gifts and drawings – you know, a right creep!! However, the teachers did not know just how competitive and scheming I really was.

There were a certain three girls in my class who in my opinion were just that little bit better than me – in some areas.

Girl No 1 was prettier.

Girl No 2 had neater handwriting.

Girl No 3 was just a little better at swimming.

So I, 'little Miss sweet and innocent', decided to teach them a lesson. On three separate occasions while in the swimming pool for class lessons, I asked for permission, and went to the toilet. In the changing room I searched through their bags and then flushed their knickers down the loo – before calmly returning to my lesson!

The real pleasure for me was seeing all the boys getting held in detention at break time because none of them owned up! (I wonder why!) But I also enjoyed seeing the three girls getting a pair of knickers from the lost property bag which were usually either too large or too small, and not very pleasant!

Well, I've come clean – will you ever be able to forgive me?

Many thanks,
Christine.

Penarth
South Glamorgan

Dear Simon and the Breakfast Crew,

I would like to make a confession about something that happened about two years ago, when I was at St Richard Gwyn high school.

I used to have a tank of tadpoles that I looked after. As all tadpoles do, they grew into tiny frogs, so I put them into a big bowl in my back garden. Sadly the sun dried them up.

I was studying biology at school, and I thought my teacher would be thrilled to study one of my dead frogs, so I put one in a small plastic bottle filled with tap water and took it to school. That day, a girl from my class (whom I didn't really like) asked me if I had a drink. I was going to say no, but then a great idea came to mind. I handed her the bottle saying, 'Sorry, but it's only water.' I only meant for her to take a sip, but she was obviously very thirsty as she drank the whole bottle, totally ignoring the frog.

I was horrified to think she had swallowed my dead frog and I had to leave the classroom as I couldn't contain my laughter any more.

So Simon, I would like to apologise to the girl in my class who swallowed my frog, and to my biology teacher as she never did get to see my frog. I hope that I can be forgiven.

from
Leah.

P.S. Please can you read out my true confession as soon as possible as I have a very guilty conscience.

Ware
Hertfordshire

Dear Simon and the Breakfast Crew,

May I confess?! About fifteen years ago I let my family eat a cake with maggots in it. (Sorry to involve more dead animals!)

When I was thirteen years old, I had a cookery exam at school. I had to prepare an afternoon tea menu, and I cooked a variety of cakes and scones, but the pièce de resistance was a Victoria sponge cake filled with fresh strawberries and cream. I got some flour from the school food store, and being very slapdash, I didn't sieve it. I now know that it must have contained weevils or maggots, because when I turned the sponge out of the tin, my friend Margo said, 'What's that on the underside of that sponge?' I looked quickly and said, 'It looks like a bit of solidified egg white.'

Then I looked closely and realised what it was – cooked maggots! Margo said that she would tell if I got a higher mark than her. So that I could hide it I cut the centre of the sponge out with a scone cutter and threw it away, covered the whole cake with piped cream, and filled the hole in the middle with the strawberries.

It looked fantastic, and I got an A grade. (Margo didn't tell – she emigrated to Australia and so my secret was safe!)

I was a normal cake-loving teenager, and my mother didn't quite understand why I wouldn't eat any of my produce that evening at home. However my Dad and my two brothers polished it off happily for dessert. Needless to say, now I always sieve flour when cooking.

I don't think that anyone suffered – they are all fit and well today. I have only ever told my younger brother who was totally disgusted, and my husband who thought it was hilarious. I'm not sure if I am sorry for doing it because it really has the makings of a funny story, hasn't it?

I feel that I should confess, though, in case Alasdair who is going to become a priest ever tells anyone else.

Love,
Eleanor.

P.S. Would you like to come for afternoon tea one Sunday?!

Dear Simon,

I thought that you might appreciate my true confession.

When I was twelve, I was not a great lover of school, especially on the days when we had P.E. I was not what you would call a natural athlete! One morning, I decided that I would rather like the day off school, so when I got downstairs I pretended that I had a stomach ache.

However, my Mum didn't believe me, and told me if I really had stomach ache then I'd have to go to the doctor's, hoping this would scare me into going to school. It didn't! I went to the doctor's and the doctor did believe me. He believed me so much that he sent me to the local Casualty Department with suspected appendicitis!

Once in Casualty, I decided that perhaps school would be all right after all. Not wanting to be found out, I told the doctor that my pain had gone. He examined me anyway. At the time I was not aware that one of the symptoms of a ruptured appendix is that the pain suddenly goes. Before I knew it, Mum had signed the consent form and I was having my normal, healthy appendix removed!

I had a fortnight off school and my Mum has felt guilty for years (I am now twenty-five) for not believing me – sorry, Mum, you were right!

Annette.

P.S. What is most embarrassing is that I'm now a Staff Nurse in the hospital which removed my appendix!

Dear Simon,

Here's a true confession that's been on my conscience now for nearly twenty years. I was a schoolboy at a not very posh boarding school. This confession is also an apology to fifty or so people, and especially the Matron.

Being keen to make a penny or two, I bought a job lot of lime-flavoured instant whip – the kind you make with milk. Other children gave me their free school milk, and I sold it back to them for a hefty profit as a yummy pudding.

After a week or so, demand for the desserts slumped. For some strange reason there was an outbreak of food poisoning. A strange stomach bug affected so many people that out of five dormitories all but one had to be hastily converted into sick rooms.

By this time there were only about ten of us not ill. No one was buying my instant whip so I started to eat it myself. I was instantly afflicted with the illness.

The full horror of what had happened became clear. Being only eleven, I hadn't been aware of the need to keep milk fresh. I'd been collecting the milk and storing it in my locker. Stocks had built up as I'd been skimping on the amount of milk I used. As the children started to fall ill I used more and more of my stocks. And because the pudding was lime flavoured they couldn't tell the milk was green. Oh well! The school magazine later reported that a 'mystery illness struck down most of the boys in the boarding house'.

I've never had lime-flavoured instant whip since.

I'm now a BBC TV reporter, so keep this to yourself.

Tony.

— 4 —

All's Fair in Love . . .

Where would we be without falling in love? Where would this book be without falling out with love? Almost all confessions I receive either start with a drink or start with a kiss. The moral is clear, avoid pubs and snogging and you will lead a confession free, if not somewhat dull life. These stories might not be as violent as Fatal Attraction, but there is no mistaking the passion on the next few pages.

Simon Mayo   Newcastle-upon-Tyne
BBC Radio 1
LONDON
W1A 4WW

Dear Simon,

Another true confession, mine is at least. I'm sure some of the ones you read out are a bit suspect. Anyway . . .

One Saturday evening I had invited my boyfriend Phil round for a meal after he had played football for the local team. A bit of a mistake on my part I now realise, as he always used to go out for a few (ha! ha! ha! a few, I said) pints with the lads after the game. I cooked a lovely chilli con carne and had it bubbling away.

I waited and waited but when he was two hours late I decided I had had enough and went down to my local for a drink with a few friends. Yes, you guessed it, there he was drinking and singing merrily while my chilli con carne burned the bottom of the pan. I was furious, but being my kind loving self, I said to Phil, 'Are you ready for your tea, Love.' He said, 'I'll be there soon.'

I left soon after that and went home. When I got home I remembered I had made a large fruit trifle full of custard, jelly and nice messy cake for pudding. Still burning from rejection I took my trifle and carried it very carefully up to the pub car park. Yes you guessed it I covered his pride and joy, his beautiful orange sports car, from top to bottom, end to end with slushy, gooey trifle. I was really proud of myself. I did a really good job and I felt much better. I have never seen such a mess before or since.

Do you think he can ever forgive me or do you think it will stop him trifling around with my feelings?

Yours for ever
Jean.

P.S. He's now my husband and he drives me to work every day, so if your listeners see someone being thrown from the car just outside Newcastle, it'll probably be me!!

Dear Simon,

This is not really a confession as I have no regrets for what I did. But it is romantic and Valentine's Day has got a lot to do with it!

When my Dad died, Mum was of course devastated and for a long time refused to accept that she would still have a life of her own. Eventually I got rather worried about her.

I was working for a small company in East Grinstead and my boss – let's call him Matthew – was a man about Mum's age and a widower as well. He saw Mum occasionally when she came to see me for lunch, and I could tell he was quite impressed. But he did not approach Mum, as she didn't give any indication of being interested. Perhaps me working for him had something to do with it too. Mum did however mention to me once or twice what a nice-looking man she thought he was.

Nothing happened for months, and they just kept on eyeing each other from a distance. After I had given in my notice to join another employer, I decided something had to be done. This was last year, just before Valentine's Day. I bought two cards, wrote a message on both, each a little different but basically saying something like: 'I have been thinking of you for a long time; it would be a great pleasure to tell you how much I really care for you, so would you like to meet me on Valentine's Day?' And I named a nice 'olde worlde' local inn where this meeting was to be and left the rest to work itself out.

When Mum got the card she looked surprised and eventually told me she had a date for Valentine's Day. When I innocently asked who this date was, she just smiled.

On Valentine's Day, I went out with my boyfriend, and towards the end of the evening I suggested we pop into this particular inn for a drink. When we came in I did not see Mum or Matthew anywhere and I thought my plot hadn't worked. But then I spotted them in a corner in the dining room, holding hands over the table and completely ignoring the rest of the world!

Mum told me later that she had received this odd card, thought it was from Matthew and therefore decided to go to the inn, but as it was obvious that Matthew was there just by chance and had not sent it, she did not tell him and she was not going to worry about it.

I have not asked Matthew's side of the story, and I have not told them as I do not think it is necessary. They got married six months ago.

With Valentine's regards,
Sharon.

Dear Simon,

Having listened to your confessions for the past few weeks, I have decided to come clean about something that has been on my mind for quite a while.

While I was at university, I met Mark, my first real boyfriend. I fell madly in love with him and we got engaged the following summer. When we left university, we both went to London to seek our fortunes, and shared a house with my best friend, Kathy. I'd set the wedding date for the following year and we were very happy. However, on Valentine's Day, he dumped me completely without warning.

I was heart-broken, but part of me felt very sorry for him because I was the extrovert in the relationship, and he was very shy. So I asked Kathy to keep an eye on him and make sure he was OK. At first she wasn't too happy because she felt he'd treated me badly, but I persuaded her that I was fine and that I had to be adult about it.

A few months went by and I hardly saw Mark, though when I did, I'd feel tearful and upset and make some excuse to leave. One night, I came home unexpectedly and went upstairs to talk to Kathy. You can imagine how I felt when I found she wasn't alone. Mark was there with her in her room!

Well, it hit the fan, but after a couple of hours of tears and anger, I calmed down and accepted that it had just happened and no one had meant to hurt me. For a few days, I acted as if nothing had happened but deep down it was eating away at me.

So, one night, when I came home and found a note saying that she had decided to spend the night at a friend's – I wonder who? – I lost my temper. Kathy had received for her birthday a beautiful set of lead crystal glasses which she kept in the top cupboard. These were her pride and joy, the start of her 'bottom drawer', as she was wont to say. I took these glasses, all six of them, went outside into the garden and smashed them on the ground, hard, one by one. Then I went into her room and took her favourite cassettes and ruined them all by pulling the tape out from inside. Then, as a finale, I stuffed her underwear under the wardrobe so far back that she would never be able to reach it! The next day, I resigned my job, left the house and went home to my mother.

I don't know what happened when she realised that the glasses were missing, but I don't think she could have failed to see the broken remains in the back yard. She is still living with Mark, three years later.

I am about to be married to the most wonderful man in the world, but I cannot rest happy until she knows that it was me who broke her glasses, and that I did it because I couldn't bear the thought of her being happy with Mark. Now I am blissfully happy and, instead of resenting her, I would like her to know that I'm glad she and Mark are together.

Yours sincerely,
Rosemary.

Dear Simon,

I'm afraid I can't give you my name, in case anyone finds out my true identity, so just call me Felix – I always wanted to be called that anyway.

My evil deed took place about eight years ago when I was at school. For years, my best friend Paul had consistently asked out girls I liked myself (he pretended they all chased him). Naturally I was getting just a bit annoyed. When we reached third year at secondary school, I suddenly saw Kate, the girl of my dreams. My rapture was such that I told Paul, and by the end of the day he had arranged a date with her.

I looked at him and thought, 'You've pushed me too far this time!'

A few months later, Paul and Kate had a tiff after he stepped on her hamster. Here was my chance – I rampaged quietly into action! I phoned Kate that night, and told her in a 'sincere Bob Monkhouse manner' that Paul was planning to render her redundant as a girlfriend the next day, and give her back the ring she had swapped with him. (I added that if he ever saw her hamster again it was going to be a flat furball.)

I consoled her tears for the next forty-five minutes, and if I had been with her I would have offered her any part of my body to cry on!

I stayed off from school next day in case it all back-fired on me, but I need not have worried. Pushing back his tears (about time too!), Paul came round to see me, and said Kate had thrown his ring into his custard at lunch-time, and had also told him 'where to go', which in this case was to a plastic surgeon to get his face re-done.

Well, I stayed with Paul in his time of need, telling him what rotters girls were (and that you can never trust hamsters). He thanked me a few hours later for being such a nice person.

So racked with guilt was I that I never ever asked Kate out. Instead I became a priest, listening to confessions, a bit like yourself. We call it repentance in the trade now, by the way. As for Paul, he married someone else's fianceé and quickly lost his hair. I gloat every time I see his receding hairline.

Yours,
Felix.

P.S. I bet this is the first time you've mentioned a hamster without it getting killed at the end of the story!

Dear Father Mayo and Sister Oxxers,

I hope I can be forgiven by you and my best friend Ellen. You see twelve years ago when we were fourteen, we were best buddies at school and had been since we were eleven. We went everywhere and did everything together. But when you get to fourteen you start to look at boys in a new light.

On the bus home from school every evening we used to see a particular boy (Steve) and we'd say how tasty he was. As we got the same bus every day, he soon noticed these two giggling girls and started to talk to us. As we were best friends we argued later about who we thought he fancied the most. Ellen was certain it was her and was getting all excited about having a first boyfriend. Now, if the truth be known, I thought Steve fancied her too but, not wanting to be thought of as the ugly one, I was adamant that it was me he fancied.

A few weeks passed and we got more and more friendly with Steve, and one day Ellen invited him to her house after school. So that day he got off the bus with us and came to her house. This is where I should really have got the message and gone home, but I didn't want him to fancy Ellen even more, after all.

There we were, all sitting in a row on Ellen's bed, Steve in the middle listening to records not saying anything. Steve then got up to go to the loo. When he'd gone Ellen turned to me and said, 'Sam, he's been holding my hand – I think he wants to go out with me!' all smug like.

Then without a moment's hesitation, I said, 'You're joking, you mean he's been holding your hand too! I think he's having a laugh. Let's tell him where to go!'

I managed to persuade Ellen that we were mature girlies and we shouldn't let him know that we knew what he was up to (luckily for me!).

When he came back, we made up some story to get rid of him. Poor bloke didn't know what was happening. Then, when he'd gone, we commiserated with each other about how awful blokes are and how better off we are without them!

So I'd just like to confess to Ellen that Steve did fancy her more, and I am the ugly one! Please rid me of guilt, Father Mayo!

Yours,
Samantha.

Islington

Dear Simon,

I have decided to lay myself wide open and seek forgiveness for what a nasty boy I was. Also, I think my sister Tessa deserves to know!

We were living near Harwich eleven years ago, and Mum was managing a local service station which had a small workshop. I was still a schoolboy, but Tessa was older and had a boyfriend called Simon (not you) who must have been already in his late twenties. Mum and Dad disapproved of him as they thought Tessa was too young for him. I disapproved of him because he called me 'Baby Brother' or 'Laddie' and anyway I thought he was the most pompous bore I ever met in my life. Everybody except Tessa disapproved of him because he smoked.

Tessa and Simon used to meet in the house while Mum and Dad were both working late. I was forced to swear silence. Tessa's room was upstairs, so they used to kick me out of my room, which was downstairs at the back of the house with a door to the garden. That way, Simon could slip out unnoticed if either of the parents returned earlier than expected. But even if Simon slipped out, the smell of cigarettes remained in my room! I got an earful more than once for smoking, and for lying, when I tried to say that I had never smoked in my life. I was praying that Simon or Tessa or both would drop dead. But they did not.

Then one night Mum was home early, saying that Tessa had promised to lock up at the station. I knew immediately that Simon was going to be there with her so I went spying. I saw Simon in the workshop smoking as usual, admiring a neat little Triumph which Dad was rebuilding in his spare time for Tessa's birthday (which was a source of great envy to me). Simon had an infuriating, 'I'll be driving this soon' expression on his face. I knew that smoking was forbidden in the workshop because of the inflammable fuels around. So I quickly took a few cigarettes from behind the till, and when Simon left the workshop I went in, burned them and dropped the ends on the floor, hoping that Mum or Dad would notice them and make Tessa explain. Then I ran away.

I didn't get far when the fire alarm started and when I turned round I saw the whole inside of the workshop in flames! The fire brigade arrived quickly and in the end there was surprisingly little damage: only the Triumph had burned beyond repair. When the fireman said a cigarette had started it, poor Simon came forward and confessed that he had been smoking in there, and so he got the blame. I said nothing.

This almost split them up but not quite. More was needed but I could not think what. Then Tessa fell off her bike and broke a leg, so she had to stay in hospital for some time. When Simon called next day I answered casually, 'Oh Tessa's not here she's gone away for a holiday with this chap David she sometimes goes out with.' (David was our cousin). There was a stunned silence and then Simon said, 'Well, ask Tessa to give me a call once she is back home.'

In the hospital, Tessa asked anxiously whether Simon had called and whether he was going to come and see her, and I answered truthfully: 'Yes, he called; no, he is not coming but he asked you to give him a call once you are back home.' I did feel bad to see how Tessa's face fell, but again I said nothing.

Then Dad decided that, since there was no Triumph now, he'd take Tessa for a holiday for her birthday as soon as she got out of hospital. Tessa readily agreed and off they went, and so it was weeks before Tessa was back home.

In the meantime Simon had not called. We never saw him again.

Am I forgiven for messing up Tessa's life? I don't think Simon would have been right for her anyway, and besides, all is well now as she is happily married and living in Guildford. She is also the mother of two adorable little boys.

Tim.

Dear Simon,

My story begins in the early summer of 1988 when my ex-boyfriend Richard (who I still had a soft spot for) went on holiday and met a girl call Kay. At the time, he was on holiday with his brother and sister-in-law, Jayne, who had always been a good friend of mine and who also gave me all the details when they came home.

Richard and Kay, Jayne told me, spent the whole two weeks together, holding hands and walking in the sunsets – this made me green with envy to say the least. She also told me that Kay was going to stay the following weekend, which was just like rubbing salt in the wound!

Anyway, their relationship blossomed and after two months Kay gave up her job and came to live with Richard. All was rosy to begin with. Christmas came and went (which I spent alone!), then in the New Year things started to look up for me.

Every time I met Jayne for a drink she would tell me all these stories of how Kay had fallen out first with Richard's parents, then with his sister, and it turned out she was upsetting a lot of people a lot of the time – except poor Richard, who seemed to remain infatuated.

Anyway this prompted urgent action from me, so a week before Valentine's Day I met Jayne after work for the usual gossip update. As we sat discussing Kay, and how the family liked her less and less and were beginning to wish she'd go back home where she belonged, I came up with the brilliant idea of a 'Drive Kay out of Chester' campaign.

The first step was to send a Valentine card to Richard. The next day I went out and bought a nice suggestive card and put the following verse inside:

> Violets are Blue
> Roses are Red
> Buy me a drink
> Then take me to bed!

and signed it 'A Blast from the Past'. I added, 'P.S. Did I leave my stockings in your car?'

In the meantime, Jayne started dropping hints to Kay that Richard might be 'playing away from home' by saying that Kay should make more of an effort to go out with the girls she worked with and to widen her circle of friends.

Kay guessed that she was meant to pick up on these hints, and asked Jayne if she was trying to tell her something. Jayne replied, 'No, of course not. I'm just thinking what you'd do if anything were to happen between you.'

Unbeknown to Jayne and me, the day before Valentine's Day, Kay tackled Richard about this and asked him if there was someone else. This accusation then turned into a full-scale row, resulting in Richard sleeping on the sofa and Kay phoning in sick the next day because she was so distraught.

Yes, you've probably guessed what happened next. Kay stayed in bed that morning, and only got up when she heard the plop of mail coming through the letter-box. Of course, when she saw the card addressed to Richard she couldn't contain herself and when she opened it – well – she was devastated.

The first thing she did was phone Jayne and tell her that her worst fears had been confirmed, and that it was obvious that Richard had been seeing someone else, and that she wasn't going to be made a fool of any longer.

Richard arrived home that evening prepared to kiss and make up, but to his horror he found the flat empty. Kay had gone and taken everything she could with her. There was a note on the mantelpiece (where the clock he'd bought her once stood), explaining that Kay now knew he had someone else and that there was no point in her hanging around. Of course, as the Valentine's card had been destroyed by Kay in a fit of temper, poor Richard didn't have a clue what had happened and was extremely hurt (oops!).

And, to this day, seeing as Kay would never answer his calls or letters, Richard still hasn't figured out why she left him. Can I ever be forgiven?

Yours sincerely,
Denise.

Dear Simon,

This is an urgent request for you to air a little confession my identical twin sister and I have been suppressing for the last three years! We were 18 at the time.

A lot of people can't tell us apart (even we have difficulty on some photographs!) and we have used this to full advantage. You name it, we've done it! Usually our games are quite harmless – that is, apart from the day Helen met Doug.

Helen had been going out with John for three months when she met Doug at work. He was six feet tall, blond, had blue eyes – you get the picture! A couple of weeks passed, and Helen conveniently forgot to mention John. Doug asked her if she'd like to meet after work for a drink. Knowing that John was working seventy miles away on an audit, Helen agreed.

Everything was fine until late Friday afternoon, when Helen's phone rang – it was John. Would she like to go out tonight, John asked. Without thinking, Helen said yes.

As she replaced the receiver, the dilemma hit her – a double booking! Helen liked Doug, but knew John would be suspicious if she suddenly backed out. Then inspiration struck. 'What are sisters for?' she thought, and quickly rang me! Being naturally devious, we thought of a plan.

I (Lucy) would go out with Doug and pretend I was Helen, while Helen would go out with John. There was a slight complication – I had already arranged to go out with my boyfriend. But, on the balance of favours due, Helen persuaded me to cancel my date. So far so good!

That evening Helen went out with John, and I went out with Doug to a wine bar. Imagine my horror when a friend of my boyfriend walked passed and said, 'Hi, Lucy!' (Remember, Doug thought he was with Helen! I should also mention that Doug didn't know Helen had a twin.) Fortunately, Colin didn't stop so I said to Doug, 'Lucy is my middle name and Colin always calls me Lucy to avoid confusion with another Helen he knows.' Doug had had a few glasses so it was quite easy to convince him!

After that Helen saw Doug a few times but never told him about me (she'd already sworn the girls to secrecy at work). Things fizzled out between Doug and Helen without Doug ever realising.

However, now has come the time to confess. Last week I started a new job. Whilst at the vending machine I heard a voice I thought I recognised calling 'Helen'. I swung round (we always answer to each other's names, because most people don't know which one they want to speak to). I couldn't believe it – Doug (the six foot, blond, blue eyed one – you remember!) My mind went racing back three years. How could I tell him my name is Lucy, and thanks for the drink?

Since it wasn't my idea in the first place, I'd like to confess on Helen's behalf. I know Doug listens to you (in the workshop), so if he has forgiven us both, can you ask him whether I can take him out to the pub at lunch time (he's grown cuter with age!).

Anyway, if we don't confess now, Doug will find out soon anyway and I don't want my new company to think they've employed someone as devious as me!

                    Yours sincerely,
                    Lucy and Helen.

Coal Aston
Nr. Sheffield

Simon Mayo
(True Confessions)
Radio 1
Broadcasting House
LONDON W1A 4WW

Dear Simon,

Mine is a double confession in that it involves two people.

When I was fifteen years of age (I am now forty-one) my best friend and I decided one Sunday night to go to my local Youth Club owing to the fact that we were skint and couldn't afford to go anywhere else. We thought we would give the lads some fresh talent to choose from. Off we went and were amazed at the number of lads who chatted us up. One particular person was called Glynn and was quite a bit older than my friend and me, and had a car. It was obvious to me that Glynn fancied my friend Glynis a lot more than he did me (this wasn't surprising as Glynis resembled a typical Scandinavian girl, long blonde hair and big blue eyes). At the end of the evening, Glynn invited us both to the Youth Club Dance the following Wednesday night.

The next day at school, Glynis and I talked over whether to go to the dance with Glynn or not. I told Glynis that I thought Glynn was too old and too old-fashioned, and eventually persuaded her of this fact, and so we decided not to go. But I was only saying this to Glynis as I fancied going out with Glynn myself, if only because he had a car. Therefore, I did not tell Glynis that I was going to the dance and turned up to meet Glynn. Glynn straight away asked where Glynis was and I lied to him saying that she didn't like him and didn't want to go to a crummy dance. Glynn believed me and we spent the whole evening dancing and laughing. Glynn asked me to go out with him the following Saturday night and I accepted.

When I saw Glynis at school the following day I did not tell her about meeting Glynn, nor did I tell her I was going out with him the following Saturday night. Eventually, a few weeks later, I told Glynis that Glynn had telephoned me up out of the blue and asked me to go out with him. I eventually married Glynn but I have not seen Glynis for over twenty years.

I would like to confess to Glynis that Glynn really fancied her, not me, all those years ago, but that I lied to both of them so I could have him for myself. Do you think Glynis will forgive me? And even more important, Simon, do you think my husband Glynn will forgive me?

Yours sincerely,
Ann.

Dear Father Simon,

Forgive me, Father, for I have sinned. I would like to use your confessional to get something off my mind. It has been haunting me for over thirteen years.

It all started at a disco. I asked a girl called Bronia to dance; at the time I was chewing a piece of gum. While we danced, we talked, so I flicked the gum into the corner of my mouth. The inevitable happened, and the gum dropped out and landed in her hair! As we carried on dancing and talking, I tried to get it out, but it just got more entangled in her hair. When the record finished I looked at her and said, as if I was disgusted, 'Bronia, someone has stuck gum in your hair.' She tried to get it out, but found it impossible, and stormed off to the toilet. She was so angry that I just couldn't tell her it was me, so I grabbed my pint and slid into the darkest corner of the room.

Now, thanks to my lovely wife I have two young daughters of my own and when they are old enough to go to discos, I will warn them about the perils of dancing with gum-chewing boys.

Simon, if you could please tell Bronia how very sorry I am, it would definitely ease my thirteen-year conscience.

Yours sincerely,
Pete.

— 5 —

All in a Day's Work

As we have seen the world of romance is full of potential disaster and this with people we have chosen to spend time with. What about spending many hours of the day stuck in the same office/lab/milkfloat/shop/hotel with those we haven't chosen. It can only end in more confessions . . . .

Dear Simon,

I am writing to you to relieve my conscience of a terrible burden. I did this terrible deed eight years ago.

I used to do a milk round, and I was doing well at it until one day as I was getting out of the van to deliver a few pints, I knocked the hand brake.

I didn't notice my mistake until I was up the drive of the house I was delivering to. I heard a noise and turned, only to see the van rolling down the hill and then crashing into a brand new car. I was literally 'up the garden path'. My boss came running up swearing and I ran down to the van in shock. Twenty-five crates of milk, a van worth £4,000 and a brand new car were a write-off.

Then I formed an evil plan. I shouted, 'There they go! I saw them! I thought they were mucking around by the van!' I then claimed to have seen two paperboys messing around by the van, and as it was dark no one was any the wiser. My boss went fuming to the paper shop and demanded that the shop owner pay for the damage.

The result was that the two paperboys who delivered in that area were sacked without wages, my boss had to wait three days for a new van and lost most of his customers, the owner of the car (who had just bought it, and got a pittance of insurance) had to buy another car (not such a good one), and I retired the next day.

I hope the car owner, the customers who got no milk, the milkman, the paperboys and the shop owner who had to deliver the papers himself for a week, can find it in their hearts to forgive me.

Yours,
Mr X.

Dear Saint Simon, Reverend Rod and Divine Diane,

The time has come to 'own up' to the horrible deed I perpetrated many moons ago. I haven't given my real name as the chap concerned is still alive . . . retired, and bigger than me.

The year was 1974. I was still in my apprenticeship, but deemed trustworthy enough to be allowed out on my own. I was training as a domestic service engineer – washing machines, fridges, that kind of thing.

The boss decided to send me to Torquay for the day, as we were short-staffed. I duly trolled up in the only van available, which was unmarked, white and totally clapped out.

Towards the end of the day, I saw another service engineer heading towards me in his very distinctive, marked service van. He slowed down and extended his right arm out of the window to signal a right turn. (He never, ever bothered with new-fangled things like indicators.) My immediate thought was, 'He hasn't seen me', my second thought was, 'Brighten up a boring day, have a bit of fun and frighten the living daylights out of Mick.' So I did a 'gimme five' handshake, at thirty miles per hour. Coo! It didn't half hurt. My hand was stinging for hours afterwards. After that, I just forgot all about it.

One week later, the lads from the various depots in Devon arranged a Saturday night out in Torquay (the bright lights of the Southwest). So, there we were, a whole group of men having a good time, when in walked Mick with his whole arm in plaster! He explained that he didn't have a clue what had happened. He recalled a glimpse of a young man in a white van but that was all. His arm was broken in two places, and to make matters worse his holiday had had to be cancelled because he was in so much pain.

Naturally, we all consoled him, and as I handed him a double Scotch, I tried not to blush or look too guilty.

All I can say now is, 'Sorry Mick, you have probably forgotten me and the incident, but if not, FORGIVE ME!!'

Yours,
Bono.

Armagh
Northern Ireland

Dear Fr Simon,

I would like to be absolved from an event which occurred six years ago, when I was a student at Queen's University, Belfast.

At weekends, to supplement my meagre grant, I worked in a local car wash. The day was long, as I started at 8 am and finished at 9 pm and the proprietor provided the meals in his own home and cooked them himself. He prided himself on being an excellent cook and was always boasting about being able to set up a mean chip. At lunch-time he would relieve me of my post and I would proceed to the kitchen where my dinner was waiting for me.

One day, it was chips, sweetcorn, garden peas and a mouth-watering lamb chop. Also in the kitchen were his daughter watching television, and the two family dogs. I proceeded to eat the dinner and cleared my plate apart from one long, undercooked chip. Being of a pleasant nature I felt embarrassed leaving this chip, so I lifted it and offered it to the Alsatian dog. Without even biting the chip, the dog spat it out. The other dog, a Jack Russell, then tried the chip but he too relieved himself of it without actually biting it. I promptly set the chip back onto my plate and finished my glass of milk.

It was then that my boss came into the kitchen and asked if I enjoyed the meal. 'Oh, I see it was too much for you,' he said, spying the solitary chip on the plate. He boasted again about his chip making and promptly put the chip in his own mouth.

I was gobsmacked! The dogs stared, his daughter swallowed hard. I asked her, 'Are you going to tell him or am I?' But neither of us ever drew the courage to. I have left now and I hear his business has gone to the dogs. Could you or your team forgive me!

Seamus.

Reigate
Surrey

Dear Simon,

Listening to your confession spot on the radio every morning I felt I must write to you to tell of a situation that arose about ten years ago.

I had been working for an insurance company in Surrey for about a year, and a friend and I were under pressure from the company to attend night-school and sit a further 'O' level in order to qualify for further examinations. Throughout the summer we were subjected to a lot of harassment from management, and for fear of our jobs, we finally agreed to enrol at a Technical College. When we arrived at the college we found that only two courses had spare places. It was a tough choice, but we felt we had a better chance of passing modern history than 'O' level Air Navigation!

We reported back to our employers and told them what we had decided. They very kindly agreed to pay all the enrolment costs, and to pay for all the books we would need for the course.

The only problem was that our class was on a Thursday night. As you know, at seventeen years old, you don't miss a *Top of the Pops* show, so after attending for about two weeks, we decided we would pack college in.

Obviously we could not tell the company, they had just paid about £75 each for us, so we decided to keep it to ourselves. When asked by management how things were going, we would always say 'yes, very well' and discuss some fictitious homework we had done the night before.

This continued until the following June. We told our employers that our exam was on June 15th and that we would need the day prior to the exam and the examination day itself off in order to prepare. The company director duly obliged, and gave us the time off without loss to our normal holiday entitlement.

I spent the time off in Bournemouth enjoying a mid-week break and my friend Ian spent two days buying clothes in Croydon. We subsequently both agreed to come into the office one mid-August morning looking miserable, saying that we had failed the exam. (We thought about giving ourselves Grade As, but we decided our bosses would want to see the pass certificate.) So, in the end we decided to fail with a Grade D.

Our employers never asked to see our certificates, and to this day, believe we spent the year at college narrowly failing the examination. Up to now no one knows the truth – are we forgiven?

Yours sincerely
Graeme.

Rochester
Kent

Dear Father Mayo, Brother McKenzie, Sister Oxenbury and Friar Tuck (or whoever the Guest Producer is today),

I hope you can find it in your Radio 1 goody bag to forgive me, for I have quite a different sort of confession to get off my shoulders. I don't think telling you will ease my guilt, but at least I can try.

You see, I served in H.M. Forces for nine years, and I was in the secret elite, the Army Catering Corps, otherwise known as Andy Capp's Commandos. We had a reputation for being the Army masters of camouflage, and this leads me to my confession.

Once, in a very elite officers' mess, I was the only chef on duty for the evening meal. I had served all the officers and was rushing to get home to my wife.

So I cleared away all the food and started to wash the tables, stove and floors – like a good chef does – when in rushed a waitress.

'Quick, Major A. has just come in!' she cried. 'What's he got for dinner?' she asked.

'Hang on, I'll just have a look,' I said, and having thrown what was left of dinner away I rushed to the fridge.

What did I find? Nothing, not a bean! 'Ah,' I thought, 'I have some food left in the pans to be washed up,' so I ran to the sink.

Too late! All the food was now in the bin, except the gravy which was on the side, and the custard which the pan washer was just pouring in to the pig bin.

Panic! What could I do? Major A. was a tyrant who had to be fed! Nothing else for it! Quickly, before all the thrown-out food got covered in the custard, I grabbed a plate and dived for the bin. Yes, I'm sorry to say, out came meat, potatoes, two veg and garnish. I washed it all under the tap, heated it under the grill, sprinkled it with parsley, and it was served with a smile by the waitress who didn't know what I had done.

And, of course, once Major A. had finished his meal, as was his custom he sent a drink into the kitchen for the chef. (Mind you that had a funny taste?!)

So, I hope you can forgive my small misdemeanour, and send me some Radio 1 goodies from your own rubbish bin! I need a large (or very very large) sweatshirt – chefs can be big fellows.

Please don't give out my name, as I may have broken the Official Secrets Act telling you this!

Yours honestly,
Les.

P.S. A.C.C. can stand for:

Army Catering Corps
Andy Capp's Commandos
Aye Can Cook
Any Clown (Can) Cook
A Complete Cremation

Dear Father Mayo,

It is now four years since I left the employ of my last company, and I have a truly horrendous confession to make.

I used to work for a company in the East Midlands, and in my office there was a young lad who I was good friends with.

This junior was a cheery chappy, highly personable, but a bit gullible. He had a habit of making everyone feel depressed, with his exuberance and his 'I want to be a star' outlook on life. The problem was, he was totally devoid of any talent!

Popular rumour had it that our boss was 'doing a turn' with one of his subordinates, a rumour which he contributed to by changing his lunch hour to the same time as her, and by inviting her into work on Saturday mornings. This was against my code of ethics (even though I didn't really have one): why should she get extra Christmas overtime when I didn't?

One day, my wife and I were out for our usual Sunday drive, and we happened to pass the home of this particular young lady. (We knew her quite well, and we knew her husband was away for the weekend.) I noticed that my boss had his car parked round the corner from her house.

I was excited about this juicy gossip, and at work the next day wasted no time in confirming their affair. I added some trimmings as well (it was nearly Christmas).

Our boss soon got wind of this and, because he lived locally, he wanted this malicious rumour quashed (in case his wife found out). So, he proceeded to get all of the staff in the office one by one and interrogated each of us to try and find the source of this calamitous rumour. However, nobody was forthcoming with any info. When my turn came, I was delighted to learn that the boss suspected everybody else but me, and it appeared he was 'digging for info'.

I followed my motto: 'let's do it to them before they do it to us', and promptly implicated the office junior.

Later that week, the junior walked into my office and told me he had been fired for poor performance (even though he had been doing the job for nearly two years). I consoled the lad and called the boss all the names under the sun, and told the junior he would be better off on the dole than working for him!

It later transpired that the boss was perfectly innocent and was having his car repaired by a mobile mechanic who lived on the same estate as the woman at work.

Office junior, will you forgive me for this atrocity? Boss, could you forgive me for nearly wrecking your marriage?

                    Yours,
                    George.

Lanarkshire
Scotland

Simon Mayo
The Breakfast Show
True Confessions

Dear Simon,

In 1980, two friends, Bob and Hugh, and I attended a Union Conference in Egham, and stayed for two nights at the local university. Bob had been suffering from gastroenteritis, and on the morning we were due to leave, he was unfortunately not quick enough in rushing to the toilet, and much to his embarrassment, soiled a sheet.

He took the sheet off the bed and at 5.30 in the morning sneaked down to his car. In the boot of his car, he had a large HMSO envelope from his work and he crammed the offending sheet into it.

On our arrival home, we stopped at a small village in Lanarkshire and ate some chips in a car park next to a Police Station, which we could see was unoccupied at the time.

Bob burst into laughter and told of his misfortune that morning. He said that he had a great idea for a laugh. He then took the large envelope from the boot and squeezed it through the letter box of the Police Station.

We drove off in a fit of laughter but after 300 yards, Bob stopped the car with a screech of the brakes. Bob turned to us ashen-faced and said, 'Oh my God, my name and address were on that envelope!'

Belated apologies to the student who lost his sheet, and to the local constabulary in Lanarkshire.

Yours faithfully,
John.

Dear Simon,

I have listened for the last couple of weeks with delight to your 'Confessions' spot. It brought to mind something which I did earlier last year, and which I thought you might like to hear!

I had a job which I hated at a small knitwear factory. I'd only been there three weeks before I realised I could not stand it anymore, they were all 'yorkies' and after just one story too many of how the supervisor's husband had held a pit prop up singlehandedly, whilst he had a broken back, to allow others to get out of the mine after an accident, I decided to take action.

Next to the men's toilets was the tea-room. I went in and opened the supervisor's sandwiches and placed some ear wax into them. At lunch-time she took them out with her, so I didn't witness the outcome. However, I did manage to feign surprise and disbelief when her tea had washing-up liquid in it, and when her radio lead had been mysteriously cut in half (serves her right for refusing to have Radio 1 on!). Furthermore we all had to have a day off when all the toilets became blocked – whoever would have put *that much* toilet paper down?

Finally, the day before I was sacked for sub-standard work, I was feeling particularly nasty. I slipped into the locker room, and seeing a coat sleeve poking out of a locker I pulled it as far as I could and promptly hacked it off with large scissors. It was the supervisor's!!

I really hated that job! And now the knitwear factory has to close. I suppose the fact that on my last day, I systematically poked scissors into the back of most of the jumpers, making a slit in each one just before they were despatched, might have had something to contribute to the factory's closure!

Yours in very bad behaviour,
Shirley.

Dear Simon,

I have a confession, which I would beg your humble forgiveness for. Actually I'll probably be out of pocket for this one. Still, deep breath, here goes:

My next-door neighbour, Philip, who still lives there, was always a bit of a joker, or at least he claimed to be. I thought I'd put his sense of humour to the test and decided to play a practical joke on him. I won't go into detail about where I used to work, but let's just say with a bit of artistic expertise I managed to concoct a piece of blank royal mint paper.

I wrote on this paper to Philip, saying that he had been randomly selected by computer to travel to the Hilton Hotel in London to perform selection interviews with twenty British celebrities, the purpose being to choose one to be featured on the back of the new 1992 £50 note. I named celebrities like George Michael, Cliff Richard, Nigel Mansell etc., etc. Philip was to privately interview each one for fifteen minutes and at the end of the day he, along with eleven other randomly selected people, would decide by discussion who the successful celebrity would be.

The letter was very specific, explaining how he and one guest would be collected and driven to Manchester Airport, flown to London, driven to the Hotel, wined and dined, and spend one night at the Hilton before being returned home in the same way. He would receive £200 spending money and a suit allowance of £50 to cover any hiring costs of dress (as it was to be formal).

On the letter I had deleted the royal mint's telephone number, and put the number of work. Philip did not know, and indeed still does not know, where I work. The letter instructed him to ring between 1 p.m. and 2 p.m. on a certain day to confirm his acceptance or otherwise of the invitation. A girl in our office was leaving the following week, and she was more than happy to take the call when Philip phoned to confirm. She just played along and told Philip his tickets would be given to him by the chauffeur when he arrived the following Friday.

I just can't believe that Philip could be so gullible. He thought quite craftily, did Phil! Instead of hiring a suit, he figured that he may as well buy one, because there was always the future. In fact, he took a day off work, bought a suit, bought his wife (his guest) an evening dress, bought a new tie, shoes, you name it. He even drove his kids, very early on the morning of the big day, to a paid baby-sitter. I know all this, because Philip told me as I was leaving for work that morning. It was so difficult to keep a straight face whilst he was telling me this story with his fresh haircut and such excitement.

I needn't go on any more. Philip tried phoning my work many times, but he just didn't make the link . . . until now! He even spoke to our M.D., but the company employs 4,000 people. Philip accepts he'd been had . . . but by who??

Sorry Philip! Forgive me?

Cheers,
Peter.

— 6 —

Crimes of Passion

In the great film 'Fiddler on the Roof', Topal ruminates long and hard with the Almighty on many issues, amongst them getting your own back. 'The good book' he ponders, 'says an eye for an eye and a tooth for a tooth, but that way the whole world would be blind and toothless'. As you are about to read the wisdom of Tevye the milkman is not often heeded.

Dear Simon,

After spending the weekend at a party with some friends in Bristol, I have decided it is time to confess a recent misdemeanour. Not because I am worried, but because my former friends were absolutely horrified that I could possibly commit such a wicked crime.

Having spent a harrowing week at our Head Office in Leicestershire, I was at the railway station, aiming to be home for 11.45 am (sorry, I mean 17.45, as per our Company regulations), when I heard a booming voice in the distance. 'Hey, boy, hey you, boy!'

I ignored the commotion, as I knew this comment would not be aimed at me. How could anyone in their right mind possibly refer to me, Dave the Rave, as a *boy*, when everyone knows I'm a *man*!

I carried on perusing my newspaper when I felt a tugging at my Georgio Armani designer jacket. I glanced across casually to my right, to see a middle-aged country lady standing there in twin set and pearls awaiting a reply. She then said, 'You, boy, yes you, boy. I'm talking to you! Look at me when I'm talking to you!' At this, I took great offence; how could any woman call me 'boy', let alone twice in the same sentence?

'Is this the train to Exeter?' she asked. My devious little mind started to tick over. 'Yes,' I replied with one of my most provocative smiles. 'Shall I help you with your bags?' 'Yes,' she said, and stomped off in the direction of the train. I placed her bags in the luggage rack, made sure she was comfortable in her seat and made my exit from the carriage to await my train.

Yes, you've guessed it, she was soon speeding not to Exeter but on the InterCity heading north, first stop Sheffield. All I can say is, no one calls me 'boy' and gets away with it.

I cannot believe my friends can't find it in their hearts to forgive me, can you? I don't care if the lady in question can't forgive me, but I know if you can forgive me, my friends will in time.

I am now referred to as 'Dave *boy*'. I don't know if I can handle this.

Yours sincerely,
Dave Boy.

Aberystwyth
Dyfed

Dear Simon,

This confession goes back to July 1988 when I was the lead singer in my school group, the Sunflower Seeds. Unfortunately, I kept on forgetting to go to rehearsals, or else I was late for them. As a result, the other three members threw me out of the group. I was very upset at this, but decided to get my own back on the traitors.

The group had a big concert in front of the school to end the summer term. As they tuned up, I hid beneath the stage waiting for them to return to the changing rooms. Once they had, I clambered onto the stage and retuned the bass, and half-cut one of the strings with my penknife, so that it would snap when played. I also knew that for a couple of songs a backing tape with thunder, fog horns and various sound effects was to be used. I replaced the tape with a selection of Beatles' oldies. Finally, I changed the sound balance so that the new vocalist would not be heard, but the drums would be – far too much!

When the band eventually took to the stage, the audience responded with rapturous applause. The Sunflower Seeds started to play, but everything seemed out of tune and the drums were far too loud. After a couple of minutes, the sound engineer corrected my earlier tamperings and the group got off to a great start . . . until the bass guitar snapped a string, and they would now have to play on without it. The crowd was getting restless and their enthusiasm was waning.

The sixth song of the concert required the special effects halfway through, but when Stu turned on the tape expecting thunder and lightning, he got 'Hey Jude' instead. This totally ruined the song, but woke the crowd up as they joined in with the tape.

The band was going to pieces now, totally unnerved, and the new singer forgot his words and froze, smiling at the audience.

Eventually, the group finished their programme twenty minutes early and left to extremely half-hearted applause from the school. Even the headmaster found it hard to give any good response to it. The next day, the band split up and to this day, everyone blames the sound engineer for mucking it all up.

Simon, I'd like to confess to the crime, although I think it was a great revenge. To the Sunflower Seeds, sorry for messing up your musical aspirations and to my replacement singer, now at Aberystwyth University, will you still speak to me?

Yours hopefully,
David.

Simon Mayo
True Confessions
Radio 1

Dear Simon,

My confession goes back twenty-one years when I was a member of a military band stationed in Malta. In the forces they have what is called a 72-hour pass, which means that you are given three days off.

Unfortunately for me I did something rather silly (which is irrelevant really) and the bandmaster (from now on known as the B.M.) revoked my 72-hour pass. This meant that while all the other lads in the band were out having a good time, I was in the cook house, peeling spuds.

I was determined to get my revenge. An idea came to me which would not only make the B.M. look stupid, but would also be very funny (so I thought).

Whilst conducting, a bandmaster uses a baton. This is a thin cane approximately sixteen inches in length, and at one end, about two inches is painted black. The other fourteen inches are white. The black section is where the B.M. holds the baton.

Anyway, I secretly removed the B.M.'s favourite baton from the little wooden box that he kept his batons in, and smeared some dog stuff on to the black part. Just enough to do the trick but not so much that you could see it.

That evening, we were to give a concert at a government function in Malta. The curtain rose and the band as usual started with the Regimental March. We had been playing for about a minute when I noticed the B.M.'s nose was twitching. He had obviously picked up his favourite baton, and was wondering what the smell was. It took all my powers to contain my laughter.

We finished playing the march and it was time to turn to the next piece of music. Now at this point some B.M.s put their baton on the music stand, but usually it gets knocked off. So most of them tuck it between their knees, leaving both hands free to sort out their music. But not our B.M. No, he always put it in his mouth. Yes, you've guessed it, black end first. It came out quicker than it went in. He threw it across the stage and walked around coughing and spitting all over the place. His face was bright red and he was fuming. He then calmly walked over to his little box and picked up one of his spare batons.

The rest of the concert went off OK, although he did give a little spit now and then plus every few minutes he would wipe his lips with his hand.

My confession is not really to the bandmaster, but more to the rest of the lads in the band. You see when nobody owned up to interfering with the B.M.'s baton, the next 72-hour pass was cancelled for everybody. OK, I lost another 72-hour pass, but it was worth it.

Do you think the lads of the band will forgive me? I'm not bothered if the B.M. doesn't.

Yours,
Peter.

Radio 1 Breakfast Show
(Confession Time!)
BBC Broadcasting House
London W1A 4WW

A Multi-purpose Confession

Dear Simon,

Eight years ago my friend, Steven, and I used to enjoy playing out during the winter time. As we both found it fun sliding on the snow we decided to construct a slippery slope on the road where we lived whenever there was snow.

One winter my friend and I were enjoying sliding down this slope, incidentally wearing holes in our pants and completely ruining our shoes – but seeing as my philosophy of life is 'what the hell!' I didn't worry. After we had been sliding down this slope for ages (which by now was very slippery), my friend's next-door neighbour came out and shouted at us both, informing us that we were a hazard to motorists. Following a heated exchange of words we decided to seek our revenge.

The revenge began by collecting my friend's mother's empty milk bottles and placing them alongside his neighbour's empties. The sight of seven or so milk bottles outside his front door looked very funny. We then decided to go one step further (or several steps as the case was) by finding a big empty cardboard box.

With this rather large box we walked along several streets, collecting all the empty milk bottles. After an hour of sneaking up and down front gardens and a lot of laughs, especially when the bottom of the box nearly fell out, we emptied the contents onto my friend's neighbour's front garden. When we had finished, we counted the empties and discovered to our delight that there were nearly 120 bottles of all shapes and sizes. This made us laugh hysterically – his front garden was covered with glass bottles and both of us had visions of a very exhausted milkman. Then we both graciously disappeared into our homes, not saying a word to anyone. We never saw our milkman again (I wonder why?) and for some time afterwards the neighbour looked at us with a very suspicious eye.

Please, Mr Milkman, wherever you are, forgive us, as it was nothing personal. If you are listening, Mr Neighbour, perhaps you could forgive us as well. I can understand that you may not want to forgive me, as I still enjoy the odd prank now and again – but 'What the hell!'

Yours collectingly,
Carl.

P.S. Dad, if you are listening, it was not some lads who threw the banger during bonfire night across two houses, three back gardens and into our kitchen, it was my friend (guess who?), who decided to drop it on the red hot cooker ring that I was using at the time. Also, nobody ever broke into our house and stole your expensive brolly and my calculator. I broke my calculator and your brolly whilst messing around, and decided to hide them – in the bonfire! So you can stop locking the back door all the time and live in peace.

— 7 —

Animal Lovers?

You are about to read what apparently are the most controversial of all the confessions – that is not my opinion but yours. The only time I can guarantee a sackful of complaints is when animals are involved . . . . cruelty to humans it seems is OK. Judge for yourself, but I can't detect an ounce of malice or cruelty in any of them.

Dear Simon and the Breakfast Crew,

I know you love getting confessions about people's pets. This one is about my mum, she collects rare budgies and mynah birds. Last year her prized possession was a £500 mynah which regularly wandered around the living room for exercise.

One day when mum was out, I was hoovering and watching TV at the same time but I looked down to see the cleaner sucking up the mynah bird.

I emptied the vacuum bag but the bird was dead and mangled. To be honest I panicked, imagining what mum would do to me. Firstly I washed off the blood and carpet fluff, but it still looked too bedraggled, so I dried it with a hairdryer and stuffed it in the cage.

When Mum got back, I said casually: 'Your bird doesn't look very well.' She still thinks the bird dropped dead from a heart attack.

Do you think my mum will forgive me?

Kevin.

Dear Simon

Yes, this is yet another dreadful budgerigar confession.

It happened twelve years ago when I was on my first job for British Telecom. I'd been asked to go and fit an extension lead in an old lady's bungalow. After I'd been there for about half an hour the old lady, who we'll call Mrs F., announced that she was going to the shops and asked me if I'd put the kettle on, saying she'd return in half an hour.

I went in to the kitchen, filled the kettle with water and put it on the stove, I then promptly forgot all about it, only going back to look twenty minutes later. As soon as I entered the kitchen I realised that although I'd turned on the gas I'd forgotten to light it, because the whole place stunk of gas. I soon got rid of the smell by opening the windows but to my horror I noticed that the budgie, who was in the cage near the cooker, had ceased to be. It was flat on its back with its claws in the air. Filled with panic, I got hold of the budgie and leant it against the side of the cage, propping it up with its bell which was conveniently hanging from the roof. Satisfied that it looked OK, I went back to my telephone extension.

When Mrs F. returned from the shops and went in to the kitchen it was only a matter of time before I heard the shriek. Running in I innocently asked what the problem was. 'It's Barry, the budgie,' she said 'He died last night and now he's back on his perch!'

Do you think Mrs F. and her deceased budgie will ever forgive me?

Yours sincerely,
Stephen

Dear Simon,

It all happened one fine sunny April day back in 1983. I was just about to leave home on Sunday morning to go and play football for the local pub team, the 'Musketeers'. I can't name the actual team due to reasons you'll see later on, suffice it to say it is in North West England.

All of a sudden, I heard a scream from Katy, my three-year-old daughter – Harry the goldfish was floating on top of the tank, and was obviously dead. My wife said I had to get rid of it before I left, or Katy would get even more upset.

By the time I had found the fish net and disposed of the dead goldfish via the loo I was ten minutes late.

I arrived at the ground and gave my apologies to the manager explaining what had happened. He forgave me, because I was his best player – and the captain.

I went out with the rest of the team and joined the kick-in for five minutes. The referee then called the captains together for the toss-up. I greeted the ref and the opposing captain, and tossed the coin.

The referee then told me that our manager had informed him of my family bereavement this morning, and there was to be a minute's silence in recognition of Harry who, he believed, had been a great sportsman and swimmer. I looked around and could see the manager and the rest of the team choking back their fits of laughter. The referee obviously believed this bereavement was of a human being and not a goldfish!

So, both teams were lined up around the centre circle and took part in a minute's silence for Harry the goldfish.

I didn't let the ref know the true story, but now my manager and I would like to confess to the referee.

The reason I cannot tell you the actual town where this happened is that the manager is now a fully-fledged League referee himself, and I'm sure he wouldn't want the F.A. to know of his past treatment of referees.

Yours faithfully,
Mike.

Dear Simon,

The time has now come to get something off my chest! It all happened about sixteen years ago when I was a young girl of six.

Things hadn't been going my way that day, and in a fit of bad temper, I threw our puppy, Patch, down the stairs, knocking it unconscious. It was only afterwards that I realised how annoyed my Mum and Dad were going to be when they found out. Luckily, my sister, who was too young to stick up for herself then, was a 'willing' scapegoat!

So, Jane, if you're listening, I'm *really* sorry that you had to spend three days locked in your room without any food as a punishment for being 'naughty'!

Thank you, Simon, for giving me the chance to clear my conscience!

Yours sincerely,
Margaret (RSPCA member).

Dear Simon,

After listening to the confessions on your show every morning, my conscience finally got the better of me and I've decided to own up to something which happened several years ago.

I was about twelve years old at the time and my father bred rabbits (large quantities, around forty or fifty at a time). He would fatten them up and then sell them to the local market. At the time I had no interest in them, other than to eat one occasionally for Sunday lunch.

Anyway, one weekend my father said to my mother, 'Don't bother getting a joint, dear, we'll have a rabbit.' Off he went down the garden to nab an unsuspecting rabbit for the pot. A few minutes later he returned. 'That saved some time,' he said. 'One of the little devils had got out of its hutch, so I've hit it on the head and it's hanging up in the shed.'

Several hours passed, and the rabbit was skinned and was stewing nicely in the oven. A knock came on the door. 'Oh, Charlie,' cried the next door neighbour, 'have you seen our Ronnie's pet rabbit – it's got out and he's ever so upset – we think it went in your garden.' Yes, it was Ronnie's rabbit that was stewing away in our oven. 'We'll have a look for it, Mrs Wills,' said my father, knowing he only had to open the oven door. The following morning my father took one of his own rabbits round to console Ronnie.

I just wanted to say, 'Please forgive me, Ronnie, for knowingly eating your pet rabbit, Bugle – he tasted absolutely delicious. I made a key-ring out of his tail – so if for sentimental reasons you'd like it, just let me know.'

Linda.

P.S. I've since turned vegetarian.

BUGLE

— 8 —

Students

A chapter to make you feel proud. A number of examples of how Britain's educated elite manage, on the barest grant cheques, to expand their creativity in to the realm of the confessional. What your career officer never told you about life in higher education.

Chiselhurst
Kent

Simon Mayo and The Breakfast Crew
BBC Radio 1
London W1A 4WW

Dear Simon & Crew,

I am writing to beg forgiveness for having such a beastly son, Jay, who is currently studying at the University of Kent, Canterbury.

We have all heard of the story about the chap who smuggled in a live chicken when he went to watch the Alfred Hitchcock film *The Birds*. At the appropriate time, he released the poor chicken from the balcony to flutter amongst the terrified audience below.

Well, one Saturday evening, Jay and a crowd of his friends decided to go into a cinema at Folkestone to see the film *Arachnophobia*. Beastly horror that he is, he took with him a packet of small plastic spiders in his pocket, and at the most scary parts of the film he lobbed the fake spiders at unsuspecting members of the audience! He thought it hilarious to listen to the ear-piercing screams!!

Please forgive me for having such a horrible son, and please, on behalf of the audience at the cinema on Saturday evening (and probably the cleaners on Sunday morning) forgive him for his perverse sense of humour!

Yours sincerely,
Mrs L.H.

Dear Father Simon,

Your 'confessional' has given me the chance to get a great weight off my chest.

Four years ago, I was at university studying for a Chemistry degree. A friend of mine on the same course, Phil, decided that he wouldn't bother coming in for the early morning lectures because he was too lazy. I, of course, went to all the lectures and would lend him my notes to copy.

Unfortunately, he kept on losing my notes so I decided to photocopy them for him instead. However, a plan started to form – why should I have to go to all the early lectures so Phil could get all the notes. So, as I photocopied the notes for him, I would omit certain important paragraphs and equations, or change them so that they were incorrect.

By the end of the first year, Phil had over two hundred pages of work that was completely wrong. The first year exams came – I passed and Phil failed miserably. He just couldn't understand it. Fortunately, he would have another chance in the October resit, so that he could go into the second year.

I saw him just before the first resit to wish him good luck and he said he felt very confident. He had been revising for about eight hours a day since he had failed. Well the results came out and Phil had failed even more miserably and was thrown off the course.

According to his last letter to me, he has managed to get a job as a milkman (lots of getting up early!). It's sad to think that he had once had aspirations of running a multi-national company.

Well, Phil, I must confess that the reason that you're not where you once hoped to be is my slightly inaccurate chemistry notes. Can you forgive me, Breakfast Crew?

> Yours hopefully,
> David.

Somewhere in Berkshire

Simon Mayo and His Crew
The Confessional
The Breakfast Show
(BBC) Radio 1
London
W1A 4WW

Dear Simon & Crew,

I have been forced to write this confession, but anonymity must be maintained as it is so bad.

Some years ago I went to Amsterdam on holiday with a friend, purchased some illegal leaves and smuggled them back into this country. That is a confession in itself, but what follows is far, far worse!

I was informed that the seeds on the leaves could be cultivated if germinated in a damp tissue and left on my bedroom window sill, so there they remained. A couple of years later, having been away at college, I was chatting to my parents about 'Mr Jones' the well-respected Headmaster, JP, Charity Organiser and all-round community 'good guy' in our town, when my mother commented how 'green fingered' he was, and revealed that she had given the seeds on my bedroom window sill to him! My spine froze. I was devastated. I imagined the headlines in the papers . . .

HEAD GROWS OWN DOPE

So please, if you are a Headmaster in the north-west of England, cut down the now twelve-foot plant with the spiky leaves – it's illegal!

This is a true confession.

Anon.

P.S. Can I be forgiven?

Stratford
London

Simon Mayo, Esq
Radio 1
BBC

Dear Simon,

After eleven years of guilt, I would like to take this opportunity to make a confession to an old college friend.

In 1980, I was sharing a flat with my friend, Mark, in Loughborough where we were both studying for degrees. As there were four of us sharing the flat, we used to have a cooking rota whereby one of us would cook the evening meal.

Mark would get very upset if any of us ever left any food on our plates, and would 'pick us up' if we left even the tiniest piece of gristle or bone. He was always telling us how fussy we were. One day, feeling a bit fed up with being constantly moaned at for being so wasteful, I decided action was necessary.

It was my turn to cook and I bought some home-made steak pies from the local butcher. For one of the pies, however, I carefully sliced off the top, scooped out the meat and substituted some other meat I'd bought the same day. Having carefully reconstructed the pie, I then marked it so as to ensure that Mark would be its recipient.

Supper-time arrived, and we all hungrily sat down to devour our meals. Nothing was amiss until Mark stuck his knife into his pie and some strange smelling juices started oozing out. We all wondered what the strange smell could be, but true to form Mark carried on eating the pie regardless until his plate was empty.

Later on that evening, Mark announced that he was going to bed early as he didn't feel particularly well. He thought that perhaps he had a bout of flu coming on. I wondered to myself was it really flu, or was it the cat food (rabbit flavour) I had put in his pie?

I am now a tax accountant and I believe that Mark works for a bank. If you're listening, Mark, will you forgive me my sins?

Regards,
Ian.

P.S. *Apparently 8 out of 10 students (who expressed a preference) prefer Whiskas!*

P.P.S. *Really enjoy the show — it's a great start to the day. Keep up the good work!*

— 9 —

It All Started in the Pub . . .

I have already suggested that many confessions I receive have to be binned on the ground of taste or legality and no more so than in this category. If you think that lot are bad, you ought to see the contents of the dustbin! If you don't already know the effect of alcohol on your powers of restraint, let the following few pages be a lesson . . . .

Rainham
Kent

Dear Simon and Crew,

I listen to your programme every morning as I love a good laugh, and I just have to put pen to paper regarding your confessional spot. I give everybody ten out of ten for confessing, which is why I must own up to the case of the missing silk dressing gown my dad once had.

It goes back about six years, when my parents, who own a pub, were invited to the launch of a new beer. It was strictly by ticket only, but once I knew Noel (hunky) Edmonds was to present the new product, I just had to go. I went on and on at my Dad to get him to arrange a ticket for me. Well, as my luck was in, I was invited to attend.

So there followed a week of frantic searching for something really great to wear. A few days before the do, the right outfit was found – a mustard and green knitted suit. All it really needed was a nice silk scarf to go round my neck. My Mum and I shopped until we dropped, trying to find the right scarf to complete the outfit, but we failed to find it. Suddenly my Mum had a brainwave.

We went back to the pub, and my Mum quickly hurried off to her bedroom and returned with my Dad's new, pure silk, green and mustard paisley dressing gown. Just the thing! We found the scissors and promptly cut the back out. That left just the collar and the two sides, which made us hysterical with laughter. Just then, my Dad came up the stairs, so we threw what was left of his dressing gown into a black dustbin liner.

Well, the scarf looked great, and the whole time we sat at the presentation my Mum and I were hysterical, because Dad had said what a nice scarf I had on, and how it matched my outfit just right.

So, really I am confessing on behalf of my Mum and myself. Sorry, Dad, but that rather nice scarf was your dressing gown. As my parents now have a pub in Surrey, it's a bit far away for him to come over and give me a good slap! Please forgive me, Simon (but not my Mum, as it was her idea!).

Yours sinfully,
Liz.

Dear Simon,

About ten years ago a friend and I went to stay with my friend's uncle in the snow-covered foothills of the Black Forest in Germany. Our host ran a small farm in a very isolated area. Whilst we were there a most unusual phenomenon occurred. Every morning, sets of regular patterns appeared in the fresh snowfall. They tended to follow an almost mathematical pattern and were looked upon by the small number of locals as the Alpine equivalent of the mysterious corn circles. They consisted of circles about six feet in diameter plus several almost parallel lines. Although a farmer, my friend's uncle was an intelligent and well-educated man, and he took great interest in these patterns, spending much time photographing them and discussing them with his neighbours. Some people trekked many miles through appalling conditions to see them. During the time we were there, the story resulted in a considerable increase in the circulation of the local newspaper!

I could not bring myself to reveal the cause at the time. We spent the days rambling through the local forested hills. Every night, to get into the spirit of things, my friend and I donned our leather shorts and walked the mile or so down the hill to the local hostelry to enjoy an evening of drink and music with the local oompah band. We are of a similar build and matched each other litre for litre when it came to the local beer. On our way back home, at the same place each night, we invariably found that we could not continue on our way without certain facilities and had to make use of nearby fields. Climbing uphill in the snow with your legs crossed is not easy. It was us who had produced the mystical snow circles!

This continued every night for two weeks. We realised after a few days that this was causing a lot of confusion, but somehow our usually sound judgment seemed to be impaired by the presence in our digestive systems of large quantities of Eurofizz.

The more time and energy that our host directed to understanding this phenomenon, the more difficult it became to come clean. I must apologise to the farmer and to his friends for the time and effort they spent trying to unravel the mystery. I must also apologise to the team of scientists from Basle University, who wasted so much of their valuable time and equipment studying it, although I did feel at the time that the use of helicopters was perhaps unnecessary! Also, my heart goes out in particular to the young student whose job it was to collect snow samples with his bare hands.

Please forgive me; the memory of this haunts me every time I go to the bathroom or walk in the snow!

Yours faithfully,
J.S.H.

Fulwood
Preston

Dear Simon and the Ready Brekie Crew,

I absolutely love listening to your listeners' confessions every morning. But it always brings back awful memories for me, because each day I realise I must confess myself. Otherwise I will never be forgiven for the horrible deeds I have done to poor unfortunate and unsuspecting people.

In October and November three years ago I had the pleasure of holidaying in the beautiful, tranquil islands of Seychelles. Then, at the end of the second week, a group of Germans arrived. I'd heard all the usual holiday jokes about Germans, and presumed I would now sample them first hand. I was wrong. The people I met were very friendly, and tried to make conversation with me on every available occasion. But, gradually, the arrival of the beach towels each morning aggravated me more and more. Now, I know that some people who have never experienced the behaviour of Germans at the beach first hand might think that I am over-reacting but as the days passed it would have annoyed even a Trappist Monk! Especially when you try everything within your power to prevent them from being at the sun loungers first!

Anyway, a few friends I'd met were flying home soon, so we decided to have a party. Half way through the evening, after heated discussions, I volunteered to get up at 6 a.m. and cover all the sun loungers with our beach towels. This would give us the satisfaction of beating the Germans.

Of course, the evening turned to night, and eventually the early hours came, we were legless! Yes, you've guessed it! I slept in till 6.30. I felt awful! I staggered down the stairs across the patio and along the side of the pool till I reached the position we were all after. Oh No! They'd done it once again! They'd foiled all of our attempts to acquire the sun beds. That was it! I was blazing! Quickly making sure there was no one around, I grabbed each and every towel available and tossed them into the pool. I then returned back to bed with great satisfaction. It's funny how much pleasure one can get by being naughty. I slept like a log, waking occasionally with the odd chuckle. Eventually I got up out of bed, slipped on my swimwear and went downstairs to the pool. This was it – my moment of accolade – the gold medal, V.E. day, even passing your driving test – all rolled up into one! I couldn't wait!

When I arrived, to my dismay all the beds were taken up by the Germans. 'Guten morgen Herr Trevor' they greeted me, smiling generously. I couldn't believe it. Who, how, when? Looking round in disbelief, I noticed all the English at the poolside bar beckoning me over. They looked very angry and disturbed; I too was fuming. 'What has gone wrong?' I asked. The reply came very fast and sharp. One of them had decided to get up at 6 a.m. to put out the towels. When they had come down later that morning, their towels were all in the pool. Fortunately, for me, they had assumed that the Germans had done this and were waiting for me to give a helping hand to sort things out!

Honestly, Simon, it was like the start of World War III. There were German jokes being passed all around the hotel, snide comments, dirty looks, fights for places on the dance floor, at the bar, and of course for the sun loungers. The poor Germans had no idea what an aggressive race the English can be!

I managed to stop the fracas over the sunbeds, put my friends on their plane, and kept the peace for the next three weeks. It was very tense and very volatile at times. I was well respected by both sides for being diplomatic, but eventually I too departed for home. I left behind me an island about to be turned into a battleground. Little did either side know the real truth. It was too risky and too late to explain that it was really me who had thrown the English holiday-makers' towels in the pool.

All this was a genuine mistake, and the real true confession is that, although I have never told anyone what happened, I can't help chuckling every time I think about it. I really am sorry. Can I be forgiven?

Sincerely,
Trevor.

A Christmas Confession

Dear Simon,

My confession take me back to 1984, a time when I had the misfortune to be a long-distance commuter. I was travelling, courtesy of British Rail, some 80 miles each day between Kent and London. It was during the years when Jimmy Savile's favourite advertising slogan, 'This is the age of the train,' seemed to us long-suffering commuters to make reference to the antiquity value of the rolling stock rather than to any special service provided.

Anyway, one fateful evening after an unusually late-night drinking session in the heart of London, I found that I had left it a little late to get home. Consequently I rushed to the station to find that the last train was about to depart. I made a dash and just managed to board the train as the guard blew his whistle for the train to pull out.

I found myself in a packed compartment and after taking a few seconds to recover I managed to squeeze myself into a seat in the corner. It was then that I became aware of a bit of a predicament into which I had inadvertently strayed. I realised that, having consumed a large quantity of liquid refreshment during the course of the evening, I now not unnaturally required the use of a lavatory. Unfortunately as my journey home on the train took a mere one hour and ten minutes, with fifteen stops along the way, good old British Rail had deemed a toilet an unnecessary luxury.

My first reaction to the dilemma was a positive one: 'I can hold it back,' I thought bravely. However, five minutes and two stops later, my second reaction was an equally positive one: 'No I can't,' I thought realistically.

By the time the train came to a halt for the third time I was in a certain amount of pain, and, in desperation, knowing something had to be done, I got off the train and started walking up the platform looking for a toilet. This was the last train of the night, and there wouldn't be another one for six hours, and so I walked uncertainly alongside the train, in case the guard started blowing his whistle. The whistle blew and I got back on to the train without resolving the problem. This time the compartment that I found myself in had just two other occupants, both city gents reading non-tabloid newspapers.

Suddenly I knew what I had to do. The time had come to take the matter firmly in hand. As we pulled out of the station I turned to my travelling companions and said, 'You fellows are going to have to excuse me, but I'm going to have a pee out of the window.'

My companions did not seem particularly impressed. One ignored me completely; the other tut-tutted and buried his head deeper into his newspaper. Unperturbed, I stood up and pulled the window down. Unfortunately the window would only open halfway, which was somewhere in the region of chest height. However, now that I was in a more resourceful mood, I solved the problem in a matter of seconds by placing my feet on the seats on either side of the aisle. This raised me to the correct level, but brought the added problem of maintaining my balance, as being up higher exaggerated the swaying motion of the train. Within seconds I almost found myself pitched back in the direction of my two travelling companions in a rather ungainly manner as the train went over a set of points. This time, I overcame the problem by leaning my head, which was now above window level, against the side of the carriage. At last things seemed to be working out, and despite the rather awkward posture, not to mention the biting December wind, the next couple of minutes or so were some of the most blissful and pleasurable minutes attainable by man.

As I stood framed in the window, enjoying this relaxation, I became aware for the first time that the train had slowed down somewhat. Out of idle curiosity, I twisted my head to such an angle that I was able to peer out of the carriage window.

Now, this is really where the confessional part of my tale begins. Do you think that those poor, innocent people who I happened to be inadvertently relieving myself over as we pulled into the next station will forgive me? Yes, I'm afraid that it's true. To my horror I saw dozens of astounded faces as we slowly drew up to the platform. I know for a fact that some of them weren't quick enough to take evasive action, and to those people I can only apologise.

A few seconds later the train came to a halt and fortunately so did I. I quickly dropped out of sight in case any of my victims came in search of the phantom sprinkler. If they did, they never found me. I remained undetected and, to my relief, the train pulled out. That was the end of my little adventure.

Once again, I would like to reiterate my sincerest apologies to the victims of my desperate act and I do hope that they can find it in their heart of hearts to forgive me.

Yours sincerely,
John.

Dear Simon,

This confession is aimed at an unknown Cornish farmer (we didn't stay long enough to find out his name) who lets a field out to campers.

Four of us, Brett, Russell, Steve and I, pitched our tent in his field one Friday, shortly before opening time.

Well, at about eleven o'clock, they poured us out of the village inn, and we were wobbling back up the moonlit lane, when Steve thought he'd sussed out a short-cut across the fields. Walking anywhere wasn't easy by then, but we climbed over the gate and set out across the grass.

Cornwall has got loads of abandoned tin mines and we'd only gone a little way when we stumbled into a flimsy fence around a very big black hole. The fields were dotted with open shafts and this one was a particularly large one.

Then someone had the bright idea of seeing how deep it was. So we tossed a stone in and listened for the sound. Nothing. So then a rock gets lobbed in. Again not a sound. So then Steve and I levered a boulder out of the ground and manhandled it over the edge. Again, not a peep.

We were determined to find out how deep it was, but there isn't a lot lying around in your average field that's going to make a lot of noise. Then Brett and Russell discovered a railway sleeper and tossed that into the void. So we're all craning forward around the edge for some sound when suddenly this chain comes snaking through the grass between us, and a goat with a clump of grass in its mouth goes flying straight past us into the hole!!

Obviously the farmer tethered the goat to the sleeper to stop it wandering down one of the shafts, but he hadn't banked on the sleeper going in first. The goat didn't even get a chance to bleat.

That sobered us right up and we left early the next day – for Devon. No mines there!

Yours guiltily,
Colin.

P.S. I don't think you'll want to broadcast this one but it might make you chuckle.

A builder friend of mine ran over a cat in his truck, stopped to see if it had survived and found it lying on the pavement, but still breathing. So he got out a spade from the truck, belted it over the head to put it out of its misery and went on his way feeling all remorseful.

Two days later there was a knock at the door and a policeman stood there asking if it was his truck parked outside.

Apparently they had received a complaint from some old dear who was watching from her front window as her kitty had a snooze when some lunatic came up, clouted her cat over the head and threw it into the hedge.

The cat he actually ran over was still wedged in the wheel arch of the truck.

End Piece

If anyone feels guilty after reading this book and would like to unburden themselves by giving me their confession they can write to me at:

Radio 1
LONDON
W1N 4DJ